Praise

'This book is a must-read foɪ ....., ... to work post redundancy (or starting in a new role) if they are feeling a touch of the "imposter" creeping in and find their self-belief to be less than optimal. The process that you will learn in *Leader Unleashed* will take you to a more confident, self-aware and resilient place and allow your competence to shine through. That can only help you in your future career.'
— **Alan Dunbar**, managing director

'One can change their world when they change their mind. In *Leader Unleashed*, Sarah Farmer helps you transform from feeling like an imposter to confidently steering your own ship. With a step-by-step process, this book will help you achieve more and feel great as you do it.'
— **Stephen 'Shed' Shedletzky**,
author of *Speak Up Culture*

'For leaders of today and those that aspire to be great leaders of the future, *Leader Unleashed* is an invaluable read, providing them with a greater understanding of themselves and helping them to inspire others. With an appreciation of what you are thinking, feeling, doing and battling, and why and how it's getting in your way, this book will help you unlock your true potential. Whatever stage you are at in your career, it will help you in your current and future roles. Reading *Leader Unleashed* will help you act and grow.'
— **Heather Butcher**, head of PR

LEADER
UNLEASHED

Become one of the most highly
valued members of the executive
team in your first 90 days

SARAH FARMER

R^ethink

First published in Great Britain in 2023
by Rethink Press (www.rethinkpress.com)

This book is dedicated to the teachers who told me I was trouble and I'd never come to anything, and the small number of leaders I've had the misfortune to work with over the years who introduced me to the real effect anxiety can have on the 'imposter' within.

Without you, I wouldn't be where I am today – thank you!

Our beliefs and actions have a lasting impact. Choose them wisely. Encourage others to fly, not fail. You never truly know what someone will be capable of.

I felt the fear and did it anyway.

Contents

Introduction

'I feel as if I have had my legs knocked out from under me.' 'My self-esteem has dropped through the floor.' 'I feel exposed and vulnerable.' 'I'm obviously not as good as I thought I was.' 'I can't afford to be made redundant twice.'

These comments, and many more, were made by highly qualified, highly competent business leaders contemplating a return to a senior position after redundancy – leaders who came to me to help them overcome their anxieties, rebuild their confidence and develop the resilience they needed to relaunch their high-flying careers. If their experience chimes with your own, or if you are having any of these thoughts and feelings upon moving into your first senior leadership role, this book will provide you with the springboard to a successful transformation.

More than 50% of new hires end in failure.[1] The majority of people do not realise that the cause lies with both employee and employer. Therefore, repeated failures become not only possible, but likely.

This book focuses on a key reason for employees' part in the 'failure': mindset. By changing your mindset, you can mitigate potential problems and have greater control of the future in front of you – the future you really want, not the one you are being dealt.

There is a widespread misconception that the more success we have, the more confident we should feel in our abilities. The opposite is often true. Instead, we can feel frustrated with ourselves and confused. We want to take on different, bolder challenges and know we have more to give, but lack the inner confidence and self-belief to do so. We can struggle to make decisions, stand up for ourselves effectively or take actions we want and need to take. We are trapped inside our own heads and waste time worrying about what might happen (and it's never something positive) that we can take forever to make decisions or are so overwhelmed with fear of the unknown that we become paralysed into inaction.

This book will show you that it is normal for redundancy to feel traumatic, that doubts and self-limiting beliefs are an inevitable consequence of it, that Imposter Syndrome is a natural reaction to it – not something to be ignored or denied, but acknowledged, recognised and managed. Those taking up their first senior or executive level position can often feel all of the above too, minus the trauma of being 'let go'.

I'll bust the main myths that surround Imposter Syndrome so that you can make more informed choices on what to do about it. I'll explain the root causes of your self-limiting beliefs and introduce you to my innovative 'Impostometer', so you can measure the extent of your Imposter Syndrome and understand the true impact it is having on you and those around you.

I will then take you through my unique five-step EAGLE system, which has been proven to help people like you (and many others) take control of unwanted patterns of thoughts, feelings and behaviours, to develop and grow into the person they want to be – one that stands tall, speaks up, makes great decisions for the right reasons, shapes their future on their own terms, enjoys the ride and quickly becomes one of the most valuable members of the executive team.

Along the way, I'll share case studies of people who have been there and done it, to give you inspiration alongside practical exercises that help you put your learning into action right away. Not all the case studies are specific to redundancy; they cover a range of examples to help illustrate the points I share.

I am no stranger to Imposter Syndrome myself. I can trace its origins back to childhood. Then when I was sixteen, my headmaster's final words of 'encouragement' to me were something along the lines of, 'You will go nowhere and become nothing.' I believed him, and screwed up my A Levels, but somehow got accepted to study a Bachelor of Science degree in Applied Chemistry. I can still remember receiving my degree certificate in total disbelief. I was honestly expecting someone to tap me on the shoulder and tell me there had been a mistake.

I went straight into a sales role in the pharmaceutical industry and worked for Pfizer and other pharma giants. I smashed my targets year on year and moved into management and then training. Enticed by the allure of money, I then moved into the world of IT, where my self-worth took a huge nosedive. I dug deep, took control, and left with no job to go to and my self-esteem hanging by a thread.

I returned to pharma, got married, had my first child and, shortly after returning from maternity leave, I was made redundant, which, although it was what I wanted, felt like a kick in the gut. I can't have been good enough in the first place or they'd have begged me to stay, wouldn't they?

Returning to work a few years later in the oil and gas industry, I created, developed and ran a worldwide soft skills development programme for industry professionals. I loved the job, but I encountered intolerable treatment by some employees and senior managers and chose to take control before it made me ill, so I left to start my own business.

This book is a distillation of my knowledge and experience as Global Executive Coach and Leadership Excellence Mentor, as well as that of my clients – leaders and entrepreneurs in a wide range of sectors. It will benefit those starting their first role as a director or C-suite executive, as well as those returning after redundancy, maternity leave, sabbaticals, ill health, etc. The tools, tips and learnings are the same irrespective of your situation; the focus is on bouncing back from redundancy (or a period of absence for another reason) so that you can exceed onboarding expectations and avoid feeling like an imposter.

Through reading this book, learning from the case studies and completing the exercises provided, you will develop the power of choice. The choice to continue as you are and get what you have always got, or to make powerful, positive changes in the way you think, feel and act that will lead you to an explosion of previously unavailable opportunities. To take flight into a new, brighter, empowering future that leads you to the life and success you want and absolutely deserve. There will be no limit to what you can achieve if you are prepared to put the work in to make it happen. You could find yourself:

- Going for and getting the job of your dreams (with multiple offers to choose from)

- Moving across the world to pursue your ideal career

- Setting up your own business after years of corporate life

- Increasing your income

- Achieving a promotion soon after starting a new role

- Growing company value fast so you can retire early

- Becoming a sought-after leader that others want in their organisation

- Being a leader that inspires followers

Even more importantly, you will enjoy the ride, and it is this increased fulfilment that leads to greater success. Then the 'magic' starts to happen, as you become open to limitless opportunities.

One thing you need to know is that for those with chronic Imposter Syndrome (that is, pre-existing Imposter Syndrome, not acute onset as the result of redundancy or other traumas), the associated self-limiting beliefs are part of who you are. Irrespective of the type of Imposter Syndrome you are experiencing, you may never be 'cured' of these engrained patterns of behaviour, but you can manage them and keep them at bay. Learning to make these new habits strong enough to overcome your desire to revert to the old ones will take a lot of practice. The potentially life-changing impact you can achieve requires hard work and determination, but once you start, you will wish you'd done it years ago.

Having this book to hand when you feel yourself starting to take the easy path (reverting to old behaviours) will help you quickly get back on track and keep heading toward the life you know you want and deserve. Most people take the easy path. Only those who are truly determined, with ambition burning through their veins, will choose the hard path and make it their reality. It takes courage to acknowledge that you need support and even more to do something about it. This book is the first step in that direction, a direction that will change everything – the first step along the path that will light you up and bring you success and satisfaction.

PART ONE
UNDERSTANDING IMPOSTER SYNDROME

In the workshops and masterclasses I run on the topic of Imposter Syndrome, I am consistently reminded that people often do not know what it actually is, let alone that they might be impacted by it. Instead, they feel that there is something wrong with them, and believe that there is nothing they can do about it.

More people than you realise are suffering with Imposter Syndrome. It is without doubt one of the best-kept secrets in the boardroom. The reason for this is that no one likes to admit they aren't coping as well as they would like, or that they have worries and fears about aspects of their role. We assume this means that we are less capable than those who appear to be thriving, not realising that most of them are thinking and feeling the same as us.

A note to all employers: as Imposter Syndrome symptoms are so prevalent, it is impossible to look to employ only those who don't experience it, and if we did, we would be missing out on some brilliant minds. The only way forward is to find ways to support employees so that they are impacted less by Imposter Syndrome or, ideally, don't experience it at all as a result of the conditions of employment. Leadership behaviours and culture are the key, not pretending the problem doesn't exist.

We aren't talking about Imposter Syndrome enough, which means that we aren't solving the problem quickly enough, which leads to even greater costs – not just for organisations but for individuals. This part of the book will give you a deeper understanding of what Imposter Syndrome is and what impact it has, as well as an understanding that can change everything if you do the work that is required. In the first three chapters, I will answer the following questions:

- What is Imposter Syndrome?

- Where does it come from and why is it so hard to combat?

- How do I recognise it and what is its impact?

As a result, you will understand your own relationship with Imposter Syndrome and associated behaviours, what impact these have on you and how you can have more control over your success, build your confidence and start heading toward the life you want instead of the default one you are living.

1
What Is Imposter Syndrome?

The most common definition of Imposter Syndrome is that it is a psychological pattern in which an individual doubts their abilities or accomplishments, often despite evidence to the contrary, and has a persistent fear of being exposed as a fraud.

It is all about confidence and nothing to do with competence. All of my clients are successful and competent in their roles. What they lack is self-belief, and it's this that gets in the way of fulfilment and potential greatness.

The key word in the definition above is 'persistent'. People who have occasional feelings of self-doubt are not persistently fearful enough for it to hold them back. It is only when these feelings overwhelm us and/or have a significant impact, preventing us from doing the things we want to do, that we would benefit from taking stock and doing something about it. That's not to say, though, that those who suffer only occasionally could not also improve their outcomes by working on their self-doubt. As you will come to learn, mindset and success are inextricably linked.

My definition is similar to the one above, but I break Imposter Syndrome down into five levels, three of which don't quite fit the accepted norm. They are not how we tend to perceive someone with Imposter Syndrome. For example, the level I describe as 'utopia' is something we aim for when learning to take control of Imposter Syndrome. This is a mindset where we have *low* not *no* Imposter Syndrome. I'll explain more on this later. The other two levels that don't fit the standard definition are 'overconfidence' and 'extreme overconfidence'. You might wonder how these could be classed as Imposter Syndrome; consider, though, what assumptions and perceptions you have about the reasons for overconfidence. One might assume these people are not particularly nice or even that they are narcissists, but what if that perception was wrong?

I've worked with many leaders perceived as 'overconfident' and discovered that behind that behaviour lay fear. Fear of getting it wrong, fear of not being good enough, fear that if they behaved more authentically, they would lose their jobs. Clearly, not all overconfidence is related to fear. Some leaders who display this trait are just not terribly pleasant people (I've met a few of those, too) or, more often, they have not yet learnt how to lead effectively. They are simply getting it wrong, perhaps because they lack emotional intelligence and the related skills that great leaders have and use often.

Anyone who is getting in the way of their own success can learn a better way and so achieve more. By success, I mean a result where everyone gains, not just one individual.

CASE STUDY: TRAPPED BY IMPOSTER SYNDROME

One of my clients, B, was head of sales and part of the senior leadership team in a failing, medium-size organisation. Having been with the company for many years, he could see exactly what was going wrong and why.

Everyone else in the SLT refused to acknowledge the causes of the business's problems and focused their efforts instead on blaming each other. After all, it is much easier to attribute blame than face up to and address the real problems.

In particular, they pointed the finger at sales. Unfortunately, B had been suffering with Imposter Syndrome for many years and it had got progressively worse as he went up the ranks. He was worried that he was playing in an arena where others were better educated and more capable than him and that, one day, he would be found out for the fraud he was. In short, he felt out of his depth.

The longer this went on and the more B's department shouldered the blame for the company's failings, the more unfulfilled he felt. He lost the joy he used to have for the job. He felt institutionalised and stuck. But leaving the industry and proving himself in another sector or even another company within the sector felt like too big a hill to climb.

As a result, he remained in his role and tried to ensure that no one noticed how he was feeling. He said what he 'should' say at meetings, becoming more and more despondent as his feelings of self-worth further diminished.

The key thing to note in the above case study is that B chose to do nothing, to allow these behaviours to continue. Know that this is a choice, even though we may not believe it to be so or try to persuade ourselves otherwise – that we have reached our peak and that growth or new opportunities aren't for us; or that we must stay as we are because we couldn't possibly earn this type of money elsewhere. Yet deep down we know that this strategy is a smokescreen, and we are sabotaging our ability to achieve what we are truly capable of in life. We may also think that we are hiding this rather well from the world. Unfortunately, as we shall see, we are in fact leaking it out of every pore, and this is inevitably being picked up by others, with varying impacts on our future.

By facing up to your Imposter Syndrome, you will reduce how much time you spend in a state of 'threat' (which impacts your cognitive function and ability to perform) and be able to look forward to the rewards of a happier, more successful, less stressful future.

The five levels of Imposter Syndrome

Imposter Syndrome affects many of us, but not to the same degree. Some are more mildly impacted, some seriously hampered by it. Understanding how it impacts you is an essential starting point. I have defined five levels to help you identify your specific situation.

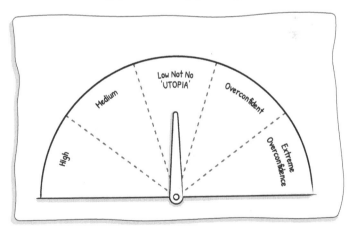

The five levels of Imposter Syndrome

All but one of the levels will have a negative impact on you, to varying degrees. The one that doesn't is Level 3, which I describe as 'utopia'. This is where you feel resilient and can operate with a non-ego-driven, unshakeable belief in yourself.

Imagine a life spent feeling like that. Aiming to be like this 100% of the time is of course the ideal, but real life isn't ideal, so knowing how to feel more in control, more of the time – especially when it matters – is the goal.

You are aiming for an improvement from whatever your base line is currently – small incremental gains lead to big achievements. Imagine how it would feel if you could improve your current state by even 10% – what difference would that make to your life?

Level 1: High (frozen)

This level typically comprises high-achieving professionals who find it difficult to accept their accomplishments. Many are perfectionists unable to settle for being 'good enough', as this feels like failure. The more success they have, the worse it seems to get. Maybe because it feels that there is more to lose, or because more people start to look up at them as 'experts' or 'heroes' in their line of work and the pressure caused by this increasing admiration and expectation starts to take its toll.

Those who find themselves at this level can be described as 'battling to thrive'. They have a consistent 'unsettled' state of mind and will not be reaching their full potential because their brain is consistently focused on what could go wrong. They are holding themselves back from the success they are capable of and the future they could have.

If you are experiencing a high level of Imposter Syndrome, you can be literally frozen into inaction. You know you want to do something but cannot find the courage, the will or the desire to figure out the best move. You may feel embarrassed or ashamed. It is hugely frustrating and debilitating, further eroding your self-esteem and self-belief.

Level 1 particularly hampers us when we are in a critical situation and our performance is under scrutiny, for example in interviews and in the first three months of a new role when all eyes are on you and results are expected, fast. Many heading back into high-level roles or starting one for the first time experience lowered resilience, confidence and self-esteem. This triggers a threat state and keeps them on high alert looking for 'danger'. For those consistently operating under these levels of fear, the impact on your mindset, and consequently on the actions you take, can be significant and detrimental to your future success.

Level 2: Medium (humble+)

It is common in the Western world to be taught that humility is a positive trait. Whether this is true or not, a level of humility is undoubtedly essential in certain situations. For example, a new leader joining an organisation who wants to create a strong 'followship' with their team from the start will find this much easier if they employ a healthy dose of humility toward those already 'in the know' about the organisation. But what I often see is clients who have taken this idea to the next level, which I call 'humble+'.

What's the difference? While being humble is possessing or demonstrating a modest or low estimation of one's own importance in the appropriate situations, humble+ is *consistently* having and showing a modest or low estimation of one's own importance *irrespective of the situation*. The intent here is different and is more aligned with being the underdog, which implies that others are better than you, more worthy, more deserving. This immediately gives them more power than you in any given situation. When we give away our power, even unintentionally (unconsciously), we render ourselves disempowered, so humble+ is not a state that will enable you to perform to your best.

Those who reside at Level 2 may easily acquiesce to the needs of others and do what others want, to avoid making necessary decisions. They may change their values and behaviours to fit in with others, often to a significant extent. This will leave them feeling uncomfortable and ultimately dissatisfied.

Those who find themselves at this level can be described as 'managing to thrive'. They may have an unsettled state of mind, but you wouldn't know this unless you knew what you were looking for because they are able to hide it well from the untrained eye and ear.

Level 3: Low (utopia)

Welcome to utopia. This is the level that allows you to go for and achieve whatever it is you decide you want, whenever you choose to do so. People operating at this level do not have a big ego; what they have is an unshakeable belief in their own worth and expertise, with a healthy amount of humility when relevant.

To reach this level, you will need to:

- Demonstrate high levels of emotional intelligence (self-awareness, empathy, emotional self-control)

- Have an open mind and effectively manage your prejudices and biases

- Be open to learning (growth mindset)

- Have a healthy respect for others' expertise

Although people in utopia will feel trepidation and, on occasion, will experience some fear when change is necessary, those operating at Level 3 know what to do about it and how to get past the block, fast. These people feel the fear, control it and do things anyway. They are mentally resilient and are often described as 'excelling' or 'inspirational'. They are more often functioning at their peak and able to realise their full potential.

You may think that you could never achieve this utopic state, but you can learn to do all the above, even in times of high stress, as I will show you in Part Two of this book. I have been working toward this state for several years and now find it possible to achieve what I want… most of the time – I'm only human, after all!

I have also seen client after client achieve these results and it is exhilarating to be part of their journey and see the difference it makes to their lives. Yes, you will sometimes get it wrong, but this gives you another chance to learn how to be and do better next time.

Level 4: Overconfidence

As previously explained, these last two levels may seem a little unusual on an 'imposter' scale, but the behaviours and beliefs driving these behaviours are similarly self-limiting, even if they present in a different way. Many people who operate at these levels have reduced self-awareness and emotional self-control and are rarely held to account for their behaviour. It goes unnoticed and/or ignored and often unmanaged for their whole career, leaving disaster in its wake.

There is a fine line between being confident without ego and being overconfident. While Level 3 describes someone with a healthy level of confidence that allows them to achieve success in an emotionally intelligent and effective way, in Level 4 we see people whose level of confidence is not always supported by evidence.

Level 4 people are likely to:

- Be less willing to accept that their point of view is incorrect

- Take more of the credit on a team project than they deserve

- Share their opinions quickly without considered thought

- Be perceived as believing they are superior to others

Note, though, that people who appear overconfident may well be masking their true fears.

Level 5: Extreme overconfidence

Clearly, anyone with perceived extreme overconfidence would not exhibit the classic behaviours associated with Imposter Syndrome. Yet I have worked with several of these characters over the years and what is surprising is that not all of them *feel* confident. Sometimes the overconfidence they display is just a smoke screen hiding their true fear of being 'found out' as an imposter.

Some have never had any training to be a leader and are operating in 'old school' ways, unchecked and unchallenged. Some have no idea that they are coming across in this way, which is purely their behavioural preference, and they have not yet learnt to be versatile. We will look at behavioural styles and versatility later in the book.

While a little overconfidence is bearable, though it may get irritating for others over time, extreme overconfidence is incredibly unpleasant to be around. Level 5 people tend to:

- Treat people with less respect and dignity than they deserve

- Believe they are right and don't ask for others' opinions

- Employ either people like them or people who won't challenge them

Level 5 people aren't often challenged, as they are deemed 'too scary'. One leader I know of who epitomises this description was well known for telling his subordinates: 'Don't praise your teams or tell them when they are doing well, or they won't work as hard.' Another would scream at his senior leadership team and tell them to 'f*** off' out of meetings if they dared to disagree with him. He saw this as 'tough love' – his team didn't share this view.

Those working with or for someone operating at Level 5 often have low trust, and behaviours tend to be replicated across the organisation. Employees will be less fulfilled and often frustrated, start to lose confidence and motivation, or pack up and move on. Level 5 people usually see higher staff turnover and high levels of absences and presenteeism and, although they may produce good results, these will not be sustained over time.

Later in the book we'll look at ways of identifying your own and others' level of Imposter Syndrome, but first we'll investigate how it arises and why it is so hard to combat.

Summary

- Imposter Syndrome affects many of us, but in different ways.

- Imposter Syndrome is defined as a persistent doubt in your own abilities or accomplishments, often despite evidence to the contrary.

- Imposter Syndrome is about reduced levels of confidence, not competence.

- My definition includes those who may be masking their fears, presenting differently but still sabotaging their future success through their behaviours and actions.

- There are five levels of Imposter Syndrome, all but one have a negative impact on oneself and others.

- The 'ideal' level to operate in is Level 3, the utopic state of unshakeable self-belief in your own worth and expertise without an accompanying ego. Here we have 'low' not 'no' Imposter Syndrome and display high levels of emotional intelligence.

2
Getting To Grips With Imposter Syndrome

In this chapter, we will explore the myths surrounding Imposter Syndrome, how we end up with it, why we can't hide it, why it's important to focus on what we really want and why a growth mindset is key to change. We will also take a brief look at how change elicits a fear response and how our response to fear slows us down, even making us grind to a halt, thanks to the negative self-talk that takes over. All of this will help when you reach the second part of the book, where you will learn how to take control of that imposter monster.

Knowing that Imposter Syndrome is so common normalises it, which in turn helps to feel more positive and hopeful about dealing with it – especially when we realise that some of the most successful people have it and still achieve amazing outcomes.

Howard Schultz, former Chairman and CEO of Starbucks, knows exactly what Imposter Syndrome feels like. He has been quoted as saying:

> 'Very few people, whether you've been in that job before or not, get into the seat and believe they are qualified to be the CEO. They're not going to tell you that, but it's true.'[2]

To manage Imposter Syndrome, it is essential to know where it comes from, which also helps explain why it is so hard to prevent. First, though, let's explode some common myths around the origins and effects of Imposter Syndrome.

Myths

In my experience, there are five main myths about Imposter Syndrome.

Myth 1: Imposter Syndrome is more prevalent in women than men

Imposter Syndrome has been shown to affect both men and women equally,[3] though it tends to be the case that more women admit to it. Similarly, more women go to the doctor than men, but this doesn't mean that they are sicklier, just that they are more likely to seek medical attention.[4]

Myth 2: Introverts are more likely to have it than extroverts

There is no concrete evidence for this, it's a myth that results from a confusion between behavioural preferences and self-limiting beliefs. What may appear to be a sign of Imposter Syndrome is often simply a more reserved (introverted) approach to communication.

Myth 3: High achievers suffer less with Imposter Syndrome

In fact, I have found the opposite to generally be true: Imposter Syndrome disproportionately affects high-achieving people, who find it difficult to accept responsibility and / or credit for their accomplishments.

Myth 4: Having Imposter Syndrome makes you more successful

Many successful people have, or have had, Imposter Syndrome, but they have succeeded *despite* it, not because of it. They either found a way to overcome it or felt the fear and did it anyway. It is not Imposter Syndrome itself but the successful management of it that can help you achieve greater success.

Myth 5: You cannot tell if someone has Imposter Syndrome

By looking carefully for the signs, asking the right questions and really listening to the answers, we can assess whether someone is impacted by Imposter Syndrome, even if it is not blindingly obvious.

Neuroplasticity and brain wiring

From the day we are born our brains are continually receiving messages from everything that we see, hear, smell, touch, feel and experience. The brain stores all this information for future reference in the form of neurological pathways, which are like a complex network of millions of motorways.

In its early years, our brain is more 'malleable' (neuroplastic) and it is far easier to change or alter a perception or belief. Think of a child who has been told something untrue. When they come home and tell you, you explain to them that this is not the truth and offer an alternative explanation. Very young children often readily accept this, and their belief on the topic changes.

As we get older, our perceptions become our reality, and our ability to question them and accept alternatives diminishes. In the case of some beliefs – for example, that it is wrong to harm another human being – this is a good thing. On the other hand, if we have come to believe that we are stupid, useless at maths, unable to make friends, or unlikely to achieve anything of worth, because these beliefs have never been contested or refuted, this becomes our truth, which can stick with us and impact us forever more. These beliefs form the foundations of Imposter Syndrome.

It is important to appreciate that not all Imposter Syndrome causes are linked to childhood or early developmental experiences. Some of us can go through life feeling confident in ourselves until we hit adulthood, when experiences at work, with a partner, or with different social groups can be the trigger.

Even though the human brain becomes less neuroplastic over time, we can, if we want to, 'rewire' it and develop new behaviours that serve us more positively and purposefully – though this takes time, repetition, determination and a lot of self-control. This is because the old, negative, success-blocking motorways have been well used. They are familiar, and with familiarity comes comfort. They are incredibly easy to access and so it is tempting to continue driving down them, as this requires less energy and effort than doing something new. Though it is not proven, it is theorised that it becomes more difficult to completely remove these pathways once we get past our early twenties.[5] But like any unused road, they will become overgrown and, over time, it will require a little more effort to go back to our old behavioural patterns that we have been attempting to avoid; it will feel more comfortable to travel down the new motorways you've built, which will get easier and smoother the more you use them.

I experienced an example of this on holiday when I hired a manual transmission car. I learnt to drive in one over thirty years ago and spent the first twenty years of my motoring life driving manuals. Even though I'd spent the past ten years driving an automatic, the ability to drive a manual without thinking was deeply embedded. The neurological pathways were strong and clear, and it took me just a couple of minutes to revert to the old pattern of behaviour required to drive a manual car. When I got home again, however, it took me several hours to switch back to the newer pattern of behaviour and I had to stop myself slamming my foot on the brake instead of the clutch. This suggests that it is easy, and so quite likely, for us to slip back into older, familiar habits when we need or want to. It also suggests that patterns of behaviour learnt in earlier years are potentially stronger than those we have used for less time, having been developed in later years.

It is also important to understand that, if the desire and need for a change we are trying to make aren't compelling, we are less likely to persevere. A desirable, and desired, outcome is necessary for anyone wanting to expedite a change initiative quickly and effectively.

Mirror neurons and emotional leakage

For those with Imposter Syndrome, understanding that we are always 'leaking' what we think and feel, through what we say, don't say, do and don't do, is a critical piece of the Imposter Syndrome puzzle. The source of this leakage is mirror neurons.[6] These are the reason it is difficult for us to conceal our feelings or emotions when performing an action; why we cannot hide our feelings of fear or inadequacy.[7] They are a type of brain cell that respond when we perform an action, when we witness someone else perform the same action or when we perform it 'virtually'. It is not just actions that these neurons pick up; they also recognise the feelings associated with the actions, which creates an emotional response in the receiver's brain.

For example, if we are scared or worried about something, such as when heading into a presentation or an interview, our actions, behaviours, gestures and words will 'leak' this information out to the people we are conversing with and trying to hide it from. It is then mirrored in the mind of the receiver. Even if they have no idea why they are experiencing whatever the feeling is, this can be enough to change the dynamic of the interaction in a negative way.

They will pick up on your discomfort, which makes them feel uncomfortable, which in turn triggers a sense of threat and a corresponding fight-or-flight response in their brain. As a result, they won't feel comfortable with you, which is not a great way to build relationships that lead to positive outcomes.

The case study below is a great example of how mirror neurons work and the problems 'leaking' can cause:

CASE STUDY: EMOTIONAL LEAKAGE

J was heading to an interview. He had been looking for a new job for months and was getting desperate and worried he would never get paid again, so he started applying for roles he didn't really want.

J was determined not to show how worried he was, but his desperation and fear of not getting a job was leaking out of every pore. It was in the words he used, the body language he displayed, the way he responded to questions and concerns. All of this led the interviewer to feel uncomfortable when what they needed to feel was confident in J and convinced that he could be trusted and was capable of doing the job.

There was nothing factually incorrect in what J was saying, but how he was saying it sent all the wrong messages. As a result, the recruiter did not progress J's application and told him he was 'just not the right fit' for the organisation.

After working with me on his mindset and influencing skills, J applied only for jobs he really wanted, showed up confident and competent and within four weeks he had received two good job

offers. His skills hadn't changed but how he felt
had – and that changed everything.

This is a classic case of Imposter Syndrome having
a negative impact on professional and personal outcomes, but the reverse is also true! J's lack of self-belief
and fear associated with getting a job made his search
harder and longer than it needed to be. This cost him
mentally and financially and put an even bigger dent
in his self-esteem. If this kind of cycle is allowed to continue, we can get into a doom loop (negative thinking
spiral), which becomes a self-fulfilling prophecy. I'll talk
more about fear and the doom loop later in this chapter.

Some of us think we can become masters at hiding our
emotions but in high pressure situations like interviews, presentations, feedback sessions, meetings
where tension is high and end-of-year reviews, this
becomes almost impossible. We are in survival mode
and all our energy is focused on that, leaving little left
to control how we are thinking, feeling and behaving.
Our emotional self-control and ability to self-manage
are reduced, with negative and sometimes disastrous
consequences.

Another key time that this survival instinct kicks in
is when we start a new role, whether this is an internal or external transition. It is even more significant if
we have been out of work for a few months or more.

The trauma of being made redundant should not be underestimated and it leaves wounds that can make performing well feel like an insurmountable challenge for many returners, exposing them to risk of another 'failure'.

The fear of another redundancy mixed with the fear that everyone and everything has moved on (even if you've only been out of work for a short time) can be overwhelming but, as we'll see as you progress through the book and learn how to develop greater self-confidence, self-awareness and essential leadership skills, it is possible to have more control over these situations than you might think.

The Reticular Activating System

Before we get into how to take control of Imposter Syndrome, it is worth briefly discussing the Reticular Activating System (RAS). This is a bunch of nerves in the brainstem, the key roles of which are regulating arousal and sleep-wake transitions, filtering out unnecessary information. In this way, the RAS helps determine how we perceive the world around us by filtering information so that we see and hear things related to what we're focusing on. The RAS is the reason why, when you come across a new word or name, you begin to hear it everywhere.[8]

In the same way, the RAS seeks out information that validates your beliefs, filtering your view of the world through the parameters you give it. The RAS helps you see what you want to see, thereby influencing your actions and outcomes. When you focus on things you don't want (a common behaviour of those with Imposter Syndrome), you are inviting your brain to look for confirmation of this. So if you believe you are bad at speeches, you probably will be. Conversely, if you focus hard enough on the goals you want to achieve, your RAS will home in on the people, information and opportunities that will help you achieve them.

Resistance to change

Growth and development are essential. Without them, humanity would have died off many moons ago. Any organisation that refuses or finds it too hard to adapt and evolve will get left behind. It is the same for people. If you want to be one of the best or, more importantly, be *your* best, growth is key. To grow, you need to develop, which requires change. We may understand this on a rational level but the emotional impact we are accosted with when change is necessary (planned or by surprise) can work against us. I'll talk more about this in Part Three of the book.

Many of us believe that we have what is termed a 'growth mindset' and yet often find ourselves denying our growth due to Imposter Syndrome, meaning that we are in fact operating with a 'fixed mindset'. We all fall into a mix of fixed and growth mindsets, a mix that continually evolves over time and with experience. A pure growth mindset doesn't exist, and it is unattainable to be focused on growth 100% of the time; accepting this is important. What you could be striving for is continual development of your ability to be open, to grow and evolve; part of this is accepting that sometimes a fixed mindset will dominate.[9]

Any time you want to do something new or different, this will present a challenge to your brain; without a growth mindset, your chances of executing the change will be low, it may even be impossible. The work you will do as you progress through this book will help you to adopt and operate in a growth mindset more of the time.

The inner chimp

The brain naturally resists change, due to fear of the unknown. Its primary function is to keep you alive, which means keeping you away from things that might harm you. It craves familiarity and consistency so change by its nature represents a threat that the brain wants to avoid. The brain will want to take the easier option, which is to continue with your current behaviour patterns, which require less energy. Making a change, doing a new thing, or trying a new way, is a harder choice that requires more energy – something the brain wants to avoid at all costs.[10]

Your inner voice, the source of the negative chatter that seeks to keep you safe from perceived danger, is sometimes referred to as the 'inner chimp'. You may have heard this term before, or perhaps read *The Chimp Paradox* by Professor Steve Peters.[11] If you haven't, I'd recommend it as further reading.

Professor Peters explains that there are two ways in which we think and make decisions:

1. Emotionally (using the limbic system)

2. Rationally (using the prefrontal cortex)

Of these, the emotional response is stronger, kicks in first and often overrules the rational, sensible thoughts we could listen to instead. Throughout this book, I will refer to the 'inner chimp' or the 'monkey brain', by which I mean the former way of thinking.

An understanding of this natural resistance is valuable for you as an individual – especially if you are embarking on a personal journey of change to overcome Imposter Syndrome – and as a leader of others, particularly when it comes to championing change initiatives. It's important to understand that change can trigger a fear response in others. To be an effective leader of a change initiative, meet people where they are, not where you want them to be. To do this, you must understand the source and nature of the fear that resistance to change stems from.

Fear and the doom loop

As explained, the brain operates with one overriding drive: to keep you alive, away from danger and make sure you have enough energy to maintain essential bodily functions.[12] I have already mentioned the well-known 'fight-or-flight' response, which is an automatic physiological reaction to an event that is perceived as threatening – whether it is literally life-threatening or merely something new / unknown.[13] In this mechanism, the perception of threat activates the sympathetic nervous system and triggers an acute stress response that prepares the body to fight, flee, freeze or fawn. One of these responses is to dilate the blood vessels so you can pump more blood to the limbs for a hasty retreat. This is marvellous if a real threat is coming our way, but the problem is that this old software our brains are running isn't great at identifying, in a complex modern world, what's a genuine physical threat and what is just different or new.

A simple change or new way of operating is enough to trigger a fear response in the brain, which is hardwired to identify danger. The perceived size and potential impact of the change does influence how much fear we feel and for how long, but even the smallest changes (or surprises), like being asked to speak at a meeting and share thoughts on a topic that you have not prepared for, can trigger a fear response and result in counterproductive thoughts and feelings.

In a *Guardian* article from 2016, neuroscientist Marc Lewis shared the results of a study on people's reactions to uncertainty.[14] He found that uncertainty is more stressful than predictable or even potentially negative consequences. This explains why we prefer to stick to old, unhelpful behaviours that have known results than risk a new way of behaving, with unpredictable consequences. Your brain will recognise known results as 'rewards', even if they aren't. But you can teach your brain to recognise new, stronger, more productive rewards. This isn't a simple matter of giving your brain new information, though, and here's why.

The prefrontal cortex has developed over time to allow us to think rationally and make sense of our evolving world. The trouble is, our emotional response (remember the 'monkey brain') to situations is five times stronger than our rational response, and kicks in faster, effectively drowning out any logical thinking about the best course of action.

People who struggle with self-limiting beliefs find it hard to take control of this negative chatter, so it remains in charge of what they do or don't do. The result is that they enter a 'doom loop', a negative thought spiral from which they find it hard to escape. One negative thought leads to another, sending them spiralling down into a belief that is no way out. My clients describe this feeling as incredibly frustrating – they know that what their mind is telling them to do is irrational and not in their best interest, and yet it is vastly reducing their ability to perform as well as they know they can. When our performance is limited through our own thinking, feeling and behaviours, our control over our future is also reduced.

Summary

- If your mindset is focused on the negative, it is working against you and your ability to be fully present.

- You are 'leaking' your fears even when you try to hide them. Mirror neurons in the receiver's brain pick up on negative emotions and these elicit a fear response in their brain.

- Change is necessary to remain competitive, but your emotional response to change and the unknown is fear.

- The fear of change (even when it is necessary) can stop you in your tracks.

- When you are fearful, you feel threatened and deploy a flight / fight / freeze / fawn response.

- Even if your rational brain tells you the fear is not real and the threat level is low, your emotional processing centre may overrule this and continue in a fear state.

- When you are operating in a fear state you cannot perform to the best of your ability, giving you less control over your future success.

3
Identification And Impact

Imposter Syndrome is incredibly common. Both men and women experience it, and it disproportionally affects high achievers and those returning to work after time out following maternity, redundancy or ill health.[15]

There have been many studies of Imposter Syndrome, including one in 2011 that found that 70% of us will experience it at some point in our lives.[16] A more recent study showed that '80% of men experience Imposter Syndrome, while a bigger 90% of women suffer from this. Despite the syndrome being this widespread, only 25% are aware of this.'[17] It can, however, be identified – both in ourselves and in others – which is the first step towards combating it. Knowledge is power – when we know how to use it.

My experience specifically over the last few years suggests that these numbers are spot on, especially amongst those returning to work post-redundancy or following time out for other reasons.

The impact of onboarding failure on the organisation

The failure rate of new senior-level hires is concerningly high. Research estimates that 50–70% of executives fail within 18 months of taking on a role.[18] This is regardless of whether they were an external hire or promoted from within.

The one conclusion we can draw from this is that, whether internally or externally recruited, it's vital that people in new roles are supported and equipped to carry out their role. For those who are moving into their first ever C-suite, senior-level role or returning to work (eg post redundancy, maternity, illness), mindset is critical, since this is when self-limiting fears, such as failure, not fitting in, making mistakes and being 'last in first out', are at their peak.

The major reasons for failure are:[19]

- 75% fail to establish a cultural fit

- 52% fail to build teamwork with staff and peers

- 33% are unclear about what their bosses expect

- 25% don't have the required internal political savvy

- 22% there's no process to assimilate new leaders into the role

The cost of a failed hire of a senior leader on a moderate salary starts at £716,000.[20] This increases with seniority, responsibility and size of the organisation. The cost for organisations to de-risk this failure and reduce the time and effort to ensure great results from newly hired executives is a drop in the ocean in comparison.

The Impostometer

In Chapter 1, I set out the five levels of Imposter Syndrome. I have also devised a simple test that can help you identify what level you are currently at and involves answering sixteen questions with a simple yes or no. You can take the test at https://impostersyndromelevel.scoreapp.com. Your answers will give you an indication of the signs of Imposter Syndrome you are showing and to what extent this is impacting you.

Your score will classify you under one of three levels: high, medium or low. Those with a very low or zero score may even stray into levels 4 and 5 – overconfidence and extreme overconfidence – although this quiz won't assess these.

Here are the implications for the five levels:

1. High: Imposter Syndrome is likely to be having a considerable impact on you and your future.

2. Medium: Imposter Syndrome is having some impact on you and your future.

3. Low: It is unlikely that you are being impacted by Imposter Syndrome in its commonly understood sense; you may even enjoy an ideal 'utopic' state.

4. Overconfidence: You may be masking your Imposter Syndrome with a show of confidence, which does not reflect your true feelings. Or maybe you are lacking self-awareness and emotional self-control.

5. Extreme overconfidence: You may not even be aware that you are self-sabotaging (a symptom of Imposter Syndrome). You believe that you have everything under control and know it all. This false belief will be impacting your relationships with others and your potential for success.

The following descriptions can give you a better understanding of the beliefs and feelings you might have at your level of Imposter Syndrome.

1. High: Frozen

- I do not believe in my own abilities and feel like a fraud.

- I believe that my achievements are accidental.

- I dislike risk, fear change and avoid it if possible.

- I am known to be self-deprecating.

- I am a master procrastinator.

2. Medium: Humble+

- I doubt my own abilities and can feel like a fraud.

- I'm sometimes risk-averse and will avoid situations or conversations that might be uncomfortable.

- Once I have made a decision, I may worry about the outcome for some time.

- I sometimes feel uncomfortable when conversing with more experienced or senior-level colleagues.

- I procrastinate and put things off when I feel overwhelmed.

3. Low: Utopia

- I believe in my own abilities and know I am good at what I do with the knowledge that there is always more to learn.

- I will discuss potential roadblocks and find ways to avoid or circumvent them with or without support.

- I acknowledge that I have played a part in the success of the projects I'm involved with and am comfortable sharing this awareness with others when appropriate.

- I believe that everyone is equally valuable and have no problems conversing with anyone at any level, in any organisation.

- I believe I can do whatever I set my mind to with the right training, knowledge and support.

4. Overconfident

- I believe in my abilities and know I am good at what I do.

- I expect success and I will happily tell others what part I played in group achievements.

- I'm vocal and contribute a lot to meetings as my experience and knowledge will help others.

- I don't think I need much self-development as I'm confident in my abilities.

- I'm usually right; sometimes others just can't see it.

Note that this level can be hard to self-identify, as you may be perceived as displaying these beliefs even if you are not aware of them.

5. Extremely overconfident

- When something goes wrong, I'll identify and inform the person to blame, and they won't do it again.

- I have complete confidence in my abilities and there is nothing left to learn.

- People do not offer me feedback and I do not ask for it.

- If mistakes are made, people aren't doing a good enough job.

- People probably find me scary and a bit unpredictable, but this keeps them on their toes.

- I would never take up professional development training; it is a total waste of time.

It is highly unlikely that anyone operating at this level will read this book or take the Impostometer quiz because, ironically, they wouldn't see the need. However, you can use this information to identify people you work with who make you feel uncomfortable and less fulfilled because they are behaving in this way. Stay and support them at your peril. You risk your self-esteem and may start to believe that you deserve to be treated poorly or that you wouldn't be better off elsewhere. Eventually, you can become a smaller version of yourself.

Keeping tally

Whatever level you think you are at, what matters is that you recognise the behaviours that you resonate with. These are clues that will help when you start to take control of your self-limiting beliefs using the five-step EAGLE system (presented in Part Two of this book).

The best way my clients have found to identify the scale of their Imposter Syndrome is to note how often, when and where particular behaviours show up and keep a daily tally. Some realise after just twenty-four hours how severe it has got for them. Others need longer. Do this for as long as you need to be clear on how things look for you.

Once you have assessed your level of Imposter Syndrome, you need to understand its potential impacts so that you can begin to mitigate them. I have found that 100% of my clients with Imposter Syndrome did not realise the full impact it was having on their life (and on those around them), or that they already had the power to change this within them. Once you have recognised these truths, you will be able to make better choices in doing something about the situation – this in itself is empowering.

My relationship with Imposter Syndrome

I would like to say at this point, for anyone suffering with Imposter Syndrome and the self-limiting and self-sabotaging beliefs that go with it, that I know exactly how it feels. My experience of Imposter Syndrome began when I was seven. What did and didn't happen next allowed my self-limiting beliefs to grow and harden to become my reality for many years to come. Having been brought up in the Jewish faith, I was sent at the age of seven to a rather 'posh' private school for 'nice girls' who did what they were told, when they were told and never questioned the status quo. Looking back and considering my personality, the chance of this working out well was highly unlikely.

To make matters even worse, I was one of around a dozen Jewish girls at the school; the others were all Christians. Back in the seventies, bias was rife – and often accepted! When everyone else went off to assembly, we were herded into a classroom together to do 'Jewish stuff' and then paraded back into the main hall for the part of the assembly that was deemed relevant to us too, while being stared at by the rest of the school.

I cannot say whether this segregation was done with a positive intent or not, but I can tell you that my seven-year-old brain figured something out fast: being different sucks. You get picked on, treated like a freak and called names; even the teachers didn't seem to like us. I could have dealt with that in two ways: quietly disappearing into a shell and hiding or getting angry and challenging the status quo.

I chose the second option, and this got me into a lot of trouble, which further engrained my belief that being different was bad. I became known as a troublemaker when really, I was just troubled. I grew up with a chip on my shoulder and found it hard to feel accepted and part of something, never quite fitting in. I think that even if I had taken option one and become quiet and reserved, the impact and consequences would have been similar, though for different reasons.

This situation continued at secondary school, where I was often in trouble for minor misdemeanours. (Like asking questions... How dare I?) By the age of fourteen I wanted nothing more to do with Judaism. I thought this might solve some of my problems. It didn't.

My self-limiting belief 'motorways' had been allowed to form and solidify. I continued to feel like I was being unfairly treated and misunderstood. The impacts on my adult life were slower promotions, fewer friends, a lot of time wasted feeling hurt, poor interpersonal relationships with some colleagues and low self-esteem and self-belief, which I thought I was hiding rather well (though of course, I was leaking it all the time).

All that has changed now. Years of self-development, coaching and counselling, and countless hours of research and practice have helped me become the best version of myself. I am happier, more successful and have amazing friends. I have more now than I ever thought possible.

Even as I write this, my self-doubt gremlins are jumping up and running amok. 'Should I be including this good news in the book? What if readers think I'm boasting?' I am not. Yes, I still get scared, I still fear change, but I understand where those feelings are coming from and know how to handle them quickly and effectively, so that I can move forward with courage and confidence. The great news is, so can you, when you know what I know and choose to use it.

All of this is achievable for you too, once you get control over the thoughts, beliefs and actions that are holding you back from what you want and deserve in life. All the things you dream of doing, saying and being will be possible. This leads to more success, plus, you'll be happier than you ever dared believe possible.

Self-limiting beliefs

Imposter Syndrome comes with a 'support army' of self-limiting beliefs that, if unchallenged, will cause you to miss out personally, professionally, financially and emotionally. Here are just a few examples of what self-limiting beliefs can lead to:

- Not asking for the rate or salary that matches your true value

- Not getting promotions or pay rises you know you deserve

- Not having the confidence to shine like the star you are in interviews and consequently losing out on jobs that could have been yours

- Being at higher risk of failing probationary onboarding periods

- Not going for the job of your dreams and sticking with one that makes you miserable

- Putting up with egotistical, narcissistic leaders who treat you badly

- Not enjoying healthy, happy working relationships

- Not setting up your own business when you really want to

- Not making great decisions quickly for the right reasons, for fear of getting it horribly wrong or suffering retribution

- Feeling that you have no right to question the direction of the organisation

- Feeling that your best is never good enough

- Over-preparing and procrastinating – 'I'll just read one more book or go on one more course before I...'

If you allow these behaviours to continue, their impact will be incalculable. They affect feelings of fulfilment, which affects productivity and, consequently, results. You can start to lose passion for your role; to feel fed up, both with yourself and those you work with; to be jealous of others who are moving ahead of you; and to start treating others in a way that prevents them from thriving too. The knock-on effect on your personal life can be considerable, as well as on the organisation you are working for. Your physical and mental health and wellbeing are impacted, with sleep disturbance, anxiety and higher frequency of illness being the most obvious signs of this. This contributes to rising (and costly) levels of absenteeism and presenteeism in the workplace.[21] If you allow self-limiting beliefs to continue to dictate your behaviour, you will be sabotaging your own potential.

Self-sabotage

Self-sabotage is a destructive behaviour that harms (or has the potential to harm) the one engaging in it. Common perceptions of 'harm' are generally related to physical and mental harm, typically inflicted by others. I have found that those who experience Imposter Syndrome rarely view the way they are thinking and behaving about and toward themselves as harmful.

Our beliefs inform our mindset, which impacts the actions we take and the results we get. But what we *believe* to be true and what *is* true are often different. If our beliefs are based on a perception of the truth that is unhelpful (eg in moving us forward), we will never achieve the best possible results. These beliefs put us into a mindset that causes us to sabotage our future.

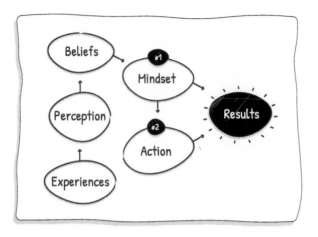

Mindset + Actions = Results

There is no doubt that those affected by Imposter Syndrome will not be performing at the top of their game, or at least not as often as they could be. This does not mean that their work is substandard. Most are massive overachievers and doing a great job, but Imposter Syndrome prevents them from feeling fulfilled, enjoying the ride, contributing more, sharing their ideas, being more creative, taking more calculated risks, inspiring others and so much more. Remember, the more time you spend in your head, the less time you can be present.

Presenteeism

A 2021 study on the global mental health challenge included an analysis of 'presenteeism', which was defined as 'working while sick'.[22] The loss of productivity that results from employees working at less-than-optimal performance levels due to poor health, particularly mental health, is a troubling phenomenon and costly for employers. Presenteeism is also a symptom of Imposter Syndrome which, though it is not classified as a mental health condition, does impact our brain health which, if ignored, can lead to issues with physical (pain, skin disorders) and mental health (anxiety and depression).[23] If your mind is occupied with feelings of frustration, of being a fraud, fear of failure, worrying about making mistakes, you are wasting limited energy resources that could be used to keep you healthy (eg fighting off infections) and mentally resilient.

You may be 'playing small', avoiding difficult conversations, shying away from making changes, not offering honest opinions or sharing ideas that may help the business grow, and much more. The lights are on but dimmed. You might think that all of this sounds trivial, but it adds up. If you multiply these behaviours across all the people in an organisation who are feeling the same way, you can see what a significant impact it has on a business and its ability to be successful.

Being consciously aware of when self-limiting beliefs and self-sabotaging tendencies are influencing your choices and finding a way past this is hugely important. The EAGLE system, which I will introduce in the next part of this book, will help you to take back control.

Summary

- We have identified five levels of Imposter Syndrome, each of which is associated with a number of observable behaviours, not to be confused with behavioural preferences like introversion or extroversion.

- You have learnt that Imposter Syndrome can lead to problems with mental and physical health.

- You have seen how, by constantly downplaying their own accomplishments, those suffering from Imposter Syndrome can sabotage their career.

- From an organisational perspective, we've seen how employees with Imposter Syndrome aren't operating effectively as often as they could be, and they are not enjoying the ride like they could (and want to) be. As a result, higher levels of absenteeism and presenteeism are possible, representing considerable costs to organisations.

PART TWO

TAKING CONTROL: THE FIVE-STEP EAGLE SYSTEM

You should by now be starting to understand where Imposter Syndrome and associated self-limiting beliefs come from and what their impacts are, but you may be wondering what you can do about it.

In this part of the book, I will take you through my five-step EAGLE system, which will empower you to manage your Imposter Syndrome. This unique process has been proven to help anyone take control of unwanted patterns of behaviour once they have decided that enough is enough and it is time to change the narrative. The five steps to achieving what you want and deserve on your terms, without the fear and consistent worry of what might go wrong, are:

1. Evaluate

2. Analyse

3. Generate

4. Learn

5. Evolve

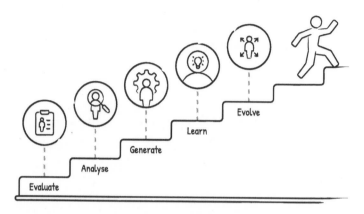

The five-step EAGLE system

This part of the book will take you through each step in detail so that you can embark on an empowering development journey and see for yourself the difference it makes in your life.

You will learn that you have more control over what happens to you than you think. You will start to take over what happens in your mind rather than letting Imposter Syndrome rule you. Your confidence will dramatically increase, and you will begin attracting what you do want, not what you don't. You will make better choices (and more quickly) that lead to better outcomes, both professionally and personally.

It is not easy to make the transition from imposter to empowered and it is often necessary to work with others who can support you and keep you account-able. The knowledge you will glean from this book is just one piece of the puzzle; only when you put your learning into practice will you see the full extent of the impact this will have on your life and career.

If you do not follow these steps, keep practising and consciously build new neurological pathways, you will be allowing your old habits and ways of thinking to keep controlling you and what you achieve, and your life will remain much as it is.

The reason the EAGLE system works is because it is comprised of small steps that pack big punches. If you are looking for a quick fix, this is not it. Quick fixes do not create lasting behavioural change. It takes hard work, determination, resilience and effort to develop and grow into the person you want to be – one that stands tall, speaks up, makes great decisions for the right reasons and is in control of their future.

I suggest that you continue to re-read, revisit and try to memorise the five steps outlined in this part of the book. Skipping steps and speeding up is possible once you get into the swing of it and have started to reap some rewards. But if things aren't working for you, you may have jumped ahead too fast and need to go back to basics. In this case, you need to slow down to speed up.

4
Step 1: Evaluate

By the time you are five, you will have learnt half of everything you will know in your lifetime.[24] This means that much of what we believe to be true is engrained in our brains at a young age. We don't think about what we see, think or feel, we just accept it. As fully formed adults, the first step towards personal growth is figuring out what is true.

People who are experiencing self-limiting feelings, thoughts and behaviours have spent hours, possibly years, unconsciously or subconsciously embedding these beliefs, which have been running unchallenged and unchecked. They are using them to stay 'safe' but in doing so have kept themselves back from the things they want to be doing and the success they could be enjoying.

As we've seen, old habits never completely die but you can turn the volume down on them so that they become less dominant. To do this, you need to be aware of them; you must know what's happening, why it's happening and what beliefs about yourself are allowing this to continue. Therefore, the first step in the EAGLE process is evaluation. This involves bringing unconscious thoughts into your conscious mind and assessing their reality.

Making the unconscious, conscious

Progress depends on a solid understanding of the deep-rooted nature of the problems that have led to your current situation. You may be surprised to learn that 95% of thoughts, feelings and actions are unconscious or subconscious. Every second, our brains process 11 million bits of information.[25] Thankfully far fewer than 5% occur on a conscious level.[26] It is believed that our conscious brain can only deal with 40–50 pieces of information per second. This means that there's a lot happening in our minds that is going unchecked.

Before any change is possible, you need to understand the true scale of the problem and the impact it is having on your life and those around you – remember, your feelings 'leak' to others and will impact them in a variety of ways. To find the truth, you need to go digging and expose the origins of the perceptions that have led to your beliefs. These old stories that we tell ourselves, stories that can hold us back, are often based on things that aren't true.

Communication style, unconscious bias and decision making

One of the key ways we (unconsciously) make decisions about others is based on their communication style preferences. To overcome this biased way of unconscious thinking, we first need to understand our own communication style preference. Our brains do not like difference. The brain's aim is to keep us safe and alive. One of the ways it does this is by noticing when we might be in danger. Anything that appears different can initiate a flight/fight response (but not always to a significant extent), which we cannot control or prevent.[27] It is an innate response to change. This gives rise to what's known as similarity bias: people who are like us, like us.[28] Similar people might have similar communication styles, but if we communicate in 'our way' with someone who is quite different from us, they will feel uncomfortable, sensing a difference.

One of the first steps toward bridging this gap is to identify our preferred communication style. Then we can consider the preference of others and (if we choose to) adapt to those needs to make our communication experience with them more comfortable and therefore more effective.

EXERCISE: An introduction to identifying communication style preference[29]

Grab some paper and draw the graph starting with the X (horizontal) axis:

Introversion   Extroversion

|— — — — — — — — — — — — — — — — —|— — — — — — — — — — — — — — — — — —|

The X axis represents how you display your energy. It ranges from introversion to extroversion.

Introverts tend to keep their energy on the inside. As an observer, we may not see it, but it is there! A great example of this is the difference between my husband and me. I'm an extrovert; he is not. At a concert, I'm on my feet singing, dancing and being, well, extroverted. You can *see* I'm loving it. My husband, on the other hand, will sit quietly taking it all in. The observer might assume, he is not having as much fun as me... well, he is. He just shows it differently. He's having fun on the inside!

Introverts can be identified as having variable eye contact and a lower voice volume; being less animated, more reflective and patient; being inclined to use silence, ask questions and think before speaking.

Extroverts tend to have fixed eye contact and a higher voice volume, are more animated and outspoken, are less patient, tell more than ask, and tend to speak before thinking.

Using these descriptions, mark a point on the X axis of your graph to indicate where you are on the spectrum of introversion and extroversion. Use your instinct; your first guess is usually the right one. Please be aware, this is just a rough guide. There are plenty of tools out there to choose from if you want to do this with greater accuracy, and I will refer to these in Part Three.

Now draw your Y axis. This represents how you make decisions.

Are you primarily a thinker or a feeler?

Those who are thinkers tend to have less varied vocal tones, come across as more formal, focus on logic first, feelings second, want to be correct and are more interested in fact than tact.

Feelers generally have more varied vocal tones, are less formal and more personal, focus on relationships first and impact on others and use tact more than facts.

Thinker
‧
Feeler

Using these descriptions, mark a point on the Y axis to show where you fall on the spectrum of thinker to feeler. Thinkers do feel and feelers do think; they just have a preference that they will unconsciously go to first.

We are all able to make decisions based on both thoughts and feelings, but which do you do first?

Now, join the two dots and you will find yourself in one of the four quadrants of the matrix. This will identify you, generally, as either a: thinking introvert, thinking extrovert, feeling introvert or feeling extrovert.

Now take a moment to consider typical behaviours that would be associated with the four main communication archetypes.

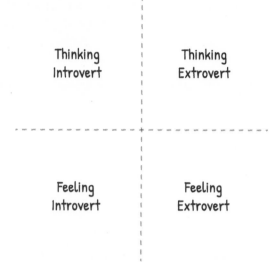

Thinking Introvert	Thinking Extrovert
Feeling Introvert	Feeling Extrovert

To get you started, here are a few to consider:

- Thinking Introvert: logical, detail focused, detached, slower paced, rational
- Feeling Introvert: amiable, slower paced, sensitive, values driven
- Feeling Extrovert: expressive, optimistic, fast paced, obvious energy
- Thinking Extrovert: assertive, fast paced, strong willed, less patient

Considering the descriptors above and how you have self-identified your communication style preference, the next step is to consider how that differs from those you work with.

The above exercise should tell you something about other people's communication needs and preferences compared to your own, plus how this may lead you to unconsciously biased thought and decision making. In Chapter 12 we will discover how adapting your communication style to another's can make a positive difference to your relationship in the future.

Evidence and reality

When you are evaluating your situation, it is important to look at how your underlying beliefs manifest. It is not enough to tell your brain what is happening; you need proof. Try this exercise.

EXERCISE: Finding proof

If you know that you have been getting in your own way, blocking your path to greater happiness, fulfilment and success, identify three specific examples of times you know that this has happened. These can be from your work life, personal life or both – you may notice some repetition and/or overlap. They could be things like:

- Times you've told yourself you wouldn't be able to do or achieve X and talked yourself out of trying, when really you were scared to fail.
- Times you did nothing because it was the easier option.

- Times you allowed yourself to be micromanaged and/or held back because you feared repercussions if you challenged it.
- Times you didn't challenge a poor or average appraisal that you felt was unfair.
- Times you stayed in a role you didn't enjoy and weren't challenged by, convincing yourself things wouldn't be any better anywhere else.

Next you can explore exactly what was happening to you when the events you have identified were in progress. This will give you clear insight into what you do and how you do it when these types of situations occur. Only then will it be possible to catch yourself in the act and stop the pattern from repeating.

Considering your examples, ask yourself these questions:

- How was I feeling in this situation?
- What was I thinking?
- How did I behave (what did I do) as a result?

Your answers should help you to see and understand the impact your choices have had on you and your ability to thrive.

Now that you have an idea of how your Imposter Syndrome presents and the impact this has on your thinking, feeling, behaviour and results, you can start to recognise instances as they occur – identifying exactly when this happens to you. You have brought these beliefs into your conscious mind, so you can no longer hide behind them.

When you do this, you will develop an ability to pre-empt the situations in which you tend to self-sabotage. You may also start to notice other thoughts, feelings and behaviours showing up in other areas of your life, so stay vigilant. This knowledge is powerful and key to this transformational process.

Some of my clients take a few minutes at the end of each week – some at the end of each day, or even multiple times a day to begin with – to reflect on and capture those moments. You might find it useful to keep a tally of how often your negative thinking pops up and holds you back. You may be surprised by how often it happens. You can do this in whatever way works best for you; the essential thing is to commit to doing it.

Below is a case study that demonstrates the power of evaluating yourself in this way.

CASE STUDY: EVALUATE

P had been working for his organisation for several years and, although in a senior position, was yet to be given the role he most wanted and deserved: a seat at the table as a director.

P had had several conversations with his CEO about a potential promotion but, although he'd proved his worth, had great end-of-year reviews and received bonus after bonus for doing an outstanding job, there was no promise of the role he was after.

P chose not to contest it or ask the hard question: 'Why am I not getting the promotion I deserve?' He just kept hoping. And nothing changed.

Eventually, P began losing the joy in his role and his lack of fulfilment began to bother him. At this stage, he came to me for help.

After P had explained his situation, we discussed his life in general and it became clear to us both that his humble, 'I'll just wait and not push things' attitude was showing up in other areas of his life, too. He described being a bit of a push-over with his friends, often acquiescing to their wishes, and his needs at home were always the last to be met. This was gradually eroding P's self-esteem.

During the coaching process, P started to accept that these behaviours were choices that he was jointly responsible for and became consciously aware of how his actions were contributing to his less than joyous life both at work and outside of it. As a result, P was able to stop hiding behind excuses and blaming others for his lack of progress and lopsided relationships. This was hard but liberating. P could now make conscious choices.

By completing the evaluation step of the EAGLE system, P became aware of what he was doing and when. This made it possible for him to take the second step in the process: analysing how it was happening and the impact it was having.

As this case study shows, hope is a poor strategy for resolving problems. We use it when we are afraid of asking the questions that will give us the answers we need – often these are answers that we fear but that will help us move forward. Knowing that we are part of the problem, and therefore have some control in solving it, is an eye-opener and often a great relief.

Of course, having hope in times of illness, etc is a quite different matter. There is a time and place for hope, but not when it comes to our career and / or how we are being treated by others. Once we stop blaming others or external factors for where we are and start taking accountability for the role we ourselves have played and are playing, we can learn to choose different behaviours that lead to different outcomes.

Until you have brought your thought process into your conscious mind and recognised how you are sabotaging yourself, how can you evaluate your behaviours and mindset accurately, or at all? Consciously capturing what you are doing and keeping a tally of how often things happen is key to being able to do something about it.

Congratulations on taking the first step toward changing the relationship you currently have with your Imposter Syndrome and associated self-limiting beliefs. Use the Summary below to reflect on what you have learnt from this step before you move on to the next stage. These moments of reflection are a great habit to get into and form part of the EAGLE ethos.

Summary

- To find the true drivers of your Imposter Syndrome, you need to expose the origins of the perceptions that have led to your beliefs about yourself.

- The old stories you tell yourself that hold you back are usually based on mistruths that you have learnt from the day you were born.

- Understanding your fears in relation to change, where they come from and the root cause of them, is essential.

- You need proof that you are self-sabotaging so you can catch yourself in the act.

5
Step 2: Analyse

In the second step of the EAGLE system, you will identify how your current mindset and associated behaviours are either contributing toward or holding you back from your ideal future.

This is important because, until you have faced the full impact of your current choices, you will find it hard to create a compelling alternative that will make new results possible. Getting a reality check on the impact of what you are choosing to believe and do is an essential step toward ensuring that you break the pattern of old, unhelpful behaviours and make way for new, helpful ones.

We have seen that our brains are hardwired to identify threats, due to their essential function of keeping us alive. This is why it is so much easier to focus on the negatives (what might go wrong) than the positives when considering what might happen in any given situation. If the brain isn't given any choices at all, it will automatically enter a 'doom loop', which will convince you to play safe and not take any perceived risks.

Before analysing the behaviours you identified in the first step, we'll first look more closely at the relationship between how we think, feel and behave.

Cognitive states

You can only adapt or modify the way you behave by consciously changing the way you think and feel. The results you get stem from the actions you take, which are impacted by the mindset you have while performing them.

Once you understand what you are doing and how your actions are impacting you, you can observe and consider the feelings, thoughts and behaviours that determine the path you are following. You can then decide to carry on with these or choose alternatives.

There are essentially three types of thought process, or states of mind, known as 'cognitive states'. These are: thoughts, feelings and behaviours.

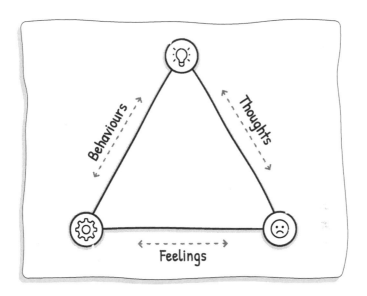

The cognitive state triangle

The way you think, the way you feel and the way you behave are all intrinsically linked, as shown by the points of the triangle. By changing one of these, you can change the others. This means that you can, if you want to, consciously choose to change how you feel, think or behave.

For example, imagine you wake up one day feeling grumpy and despondent. You can't change the fact that you have woken up this way, it's already happened. What you do next is what counts, you can choose to allow this state of mind to continue or do something to change it. When this happens to me, I put some music on and dance for five minutes (while getting withering looks from the kids). This changes my behaviour and then my mood starts to lift, my thoughts change, and I end up feeling and 'doing' better as a result. It doesn't have to be dancing, maybe a brisk walk, going to the gym, meditation, shopping, or something else will work for you.

In step two of the EAGLE system, Analyse, we will delve further into your negative thinking and corresponding feelings and behaviour, and explore the link between the consequences and opportuntities that arise from this. Imposter Syndrome is the result of persistent negative thinking, feelings and behavioural patterns, some of which you will have identified in the first step of the EAGLE system. Now we're going to look at what impact these have.

EXERCISE: Understanding impact

Using the examples from the previous chapter, where you evaluated your self-limiting beliefs and identified what experiences these have led to in your life, take each in turn and answer the questions below. Write your answers down – seeing them in written form has a much stronger impact and you can keep them for future reference when you need a reminder.

What impact does/did this behaviour/ belief have on you?

The way we live our lives always has impact. For those suffering with Imposter Syndrome, the impacts on their mental and physical health can be considerable, from sleep disturbance (caused by anxiety related to Imposter Syndrome) and illness to feelings of disappointment, lack of motivation and fulfilment. When you are not operating at your full potential, this will likely have an impact on your career and therefore your finances – missed bonuses, lost clients, smaller deals, fewer promotion opportunities and job offers. What impact can you see in your life of your negative thoughts, feelings and behaviours?

As John Donne famously said, 'No man is an island, entire of itself; every man is a piece of the continent, a part of the main.'[30] How we behave always has consequences for those around us. With that in mind, consider the next question. Take your time and think widely; it's important to get the full picture at this stage of the process.

Who else is/was impacted by the way you felt, thought and behaved in this situation, and how?

Consider your friends, partner, children, as well as your work colleagues, customers, clients and others. Acknowledging that your choices don't only impact you but also the lives of others is necessary to help you commit to lasting behavioural change. The more reasons for change you can find, the better the fight you can put up against your innate fear of change, which could otherwise keep you stuck in a rut.

After doing this piece of work, it became apparent to one of my clients how much his lack of fulfilment, obsessive working patterns and fear of failure were negatively impacting his team. He had known this deep down for some time, but admitting it, talking about it and exposing it in full technicolour had quite an impact on him, and it gave him the energy to do something about it.

What is niggling in the back of your mind that you need to openly admit to yourself?

You have now identified your negative thoughts, feelings and behaviours and noted the situations where they tend to show up in your life and the impact they have. The final part of your analysis is designed to get to grips with the purpose behind your self-limiting and self-sabotaging behaviours.

EXERCISE: Finding the source

The purpose of this exercise is to consider the behaviours, thoughts and feelings you have identified as problematic and identify what purpose they are serving and how they help you. This may seem a strange task. Surely they serve no purpose; they don't help you at all. But if you are doing something that is holding you back, ask yourself whether this is in fact a safety mechanism, protecting you from something that you fear.

If these behaviours are stopping you from doing something new or challenging, your brain will deem this to be helpful, as it is protecting you from what you fear – failure, looking a fool, being found to be a fraud. In this case, ask yourself:

What are these thought processes and patterns of behaviour keeping me 'safe' from?

Understanding where your feelings and actions are coming from and the beliefs they are associated with will allow you to quickly identify situations where they might arise in the future.

Now consider these situations and ask yourself:

Is there a real danger to my life or is this just my brain's way of keeping me safe from harm and conserving my energy?

The chances are that none of the situations in which you had these self-limiting, self-sabotaging thoughts and feelings were life-threatening and necessitated a 'stay safe' response. Catching yourself in the act and reminding yourself of this fact will allow you to break out of these limiting cognitive states faster and with less negative impact on your time and energy, allowing you to focus on what you need to do and can do instead. With this knowledge, you are in a position to choose whether you want to keep doing what you have always done and keep getting the same results, or try another way.

Once you are ready to choose another way, you can progress to the next step of the system, where you will learn to create a whole new world for yourself – one you enjoy more and in which you get far better results.

To help put this step into context, below is an example of how it looks in real life.

CASE STUDY: ANALYSE

R, who was living in a foreign country away from family and friends, came to me because she was exhausted, fed up, working crazy hours and not getting promoted. She rarely saw her two young children as she was working until 10pm most nights, about which she felt terribly guilty. Her relationship with her husband was unsurprisingly impacted; he had become the primary care provider and she rarely got to spend any quality time with him or her children.

R was a high achiever who had never failed at anything in her life. But the harder she worked, the less fulfilled she became. She had an amazing ability to see the potential downside in everything and her 'doom loop' thinking was getting worse. She knew that things would never get better in her current job. The organisation she worked in was male-dominated, archaic and expected employees to work long hours.

R had no friends outside of work colleagues and no social life to speak of. The country she lived in was so hot that she spent most of her time in air-conditioned buildings. Her extended family never visited as it was too far and too expensive for them to travel to her and she never had time to go and see them. She missed them terribly.

This situation was having an impact on every aspect of R's life. Though only in her forties, she was starting to have problems with her heart. Her blood pressure was dangerously high and she was on medication to control it. Her sleep was impacted, which often left her exhausted before she started the day and panic attacks were becoming a regular occurrence. Her mood was generally low and her ability to have fun, smile and enjoy any aspect of her life was disappearing.

She knew that she would have to leave the country in the foreseeable future, it was just a question of when. She knew that the older her kids got, the harder this would be.

What was stopping her from breaking free of this life?

You probably know the answer by now. Fear. Fear of looking like a failure, fear of not finding another job, fear of change, fear of everything that could go wrong once she made the decision to move. To R, everything was down to her; she was ultimately responsible for the whole family's welfare. This was one heck of a burden to carry on top of her fears and health concerns. It was no surprise that she was paralysed into inaction.

Once we had evaluated how she was feeling, what she was thinking and the associated behaviours (Step 1), she became more conscious of these patterns and could see when she was repeating them. When we moved on to Step 2 (analysis), R explored these patterns of behaviour and realised how they were 'helping' by holding her back from making the hard choices she needed to make for herself and her family. It became clear to her that doing nothing was more dangerous than doing something, because the impact of her behaviours spread far wider and deeper than she had realised or wanted to acknowledge.

Seeing the magnitude of the impact that her inaction was having, R realised that it could not continue without risking not only her relationship with her family but also her own life. It was the wake-up call she needed to start focusing on what she could do to change things.

With consistent support, she found the strength and determination to try a different approach and we started to implement the next part of the EAGLE system, where the focus is on the positives and possibilities of what *could be* and how to make that a reality. Had we jumped to Step 3 (Generate) too soon, we would certainly have failed. It is hard for someone who is entrenched in unhelpful behavioural patterns to accept what is possible. First knowing the causes of those behaviours, seeing them in action and feeling the impacts they have, is essential.

Summary

- You can change the way you feel by changing the way you think, which will change the way you behave.

- If your mind is caught up in unhelpful and self-limiting thoughts and behaviours, you cannot operate in an optimal high-performance state.

- By assessing your cognitive state you can see more clearly the feelings, thoughts and behaviours that determine the path you are following.

- The results you get are determined by the actions you take, which are influenced by your mindset.

- Your actions will be impacting others. Knowing this and understanding the degree and nature of the impact you are having on others can help you grasp the scale and urgency of the problem.

- Understanding how your brain works for and against you helps to expedite behavioural change.

- Until you accept the part you are playing in your situation and the full impact your mindset is having on everyone around you, it is hard to commit to a different approach.

6
Step 3: Generate

You are now at the halfway point of the EAGLE system. This is where you will start making brain 'updates' that will help you change your thinking, feelings and behaviour for the better. At this point, you will have got to grips with the scale of the problems caused by your Imposter Syndrome and the impact it is having on you and those around you. You may have had some lightbulb moments as you probed into the causes and triggers of your Imposter Syndrome. These will be extremely helpful as you work through this step.

Rewiring your brain

We are now moving into the phase of the process where you consider what is possible, where you start generating your new belief system. The old one was packed full of negativity that served the purpose of keeping you stuck in your safety zone. For everything that you were choosing not to do or say and for all the opportunities you chose not to take further, there was a set of beliefs that you were clinging to, to keep yourself safe from the potential danger that a new way of being could bring. Though these beliefs were based on perceptions and mistruths with little to no evidence, they formed your reality and shaped your thinking, feelings and actions.

This shows you how much control you can have over your future. If you can use unhelpful, limiting beliefs to determine your actions, you are perfectly capable of choosing a different set of beliefs, ones that are helpful and liberating, and using them to determine different actions and so get different results. It's time now to say goodbye to those old beliefs and behaviours and start focusing on new ones that will give you what you want. It is as simple as it sounds, but beware: your 'inner chimp' (see Chapter 2 on resistance to change) may play havoc with you here, giving you all sorts of reasons why this is not a good idea, which can slow your progression toward stronger self-belief or even stop it in its tracks.

To create new truths, new beliefs about yourself, start by focusing on the life you could be living if you weren't being held back by negative thoughts, feelings and actions. Ask yourself:

- What am I best at?

- What am I passionate about?

- What are my core values?

- If I had an unshakeable belief that I was capable of anything, what would I do?

- How much do I need to earn to live my best life?

- Would this make me happier and more fulfilled than I am right now?

Sitting underneath all of your answers will be your core values; an authentic vision for your future will be aligned with these. If, after answering these questions, you can identify a professional role or career path that combines what you are best at and what you are passionate about with a remuneration that will enable you to lead your best life, then you have found your perfect job.

To help you envisage it, let's delve a little deeper into this possible future.

EXERCISE: Future pacing

Imagine you were living your ideal life. Ask yourself:

- What problems would it solve?
- How would it make me feel?
- Who else would benefit and how?

- How much would I be earning?
- Where would I be living?
- Who would I be spending my time with?
- What would others be saying about me?
- How would I be treated?
- What would I be saying about myself?
- What else would I be doing (hobbies, etc)?

Be wildly creative with this vision and see where your mind takes you, experience and capture everything in detail. This 'future pacing' helps your brain to 'experience' what it is you want through the power of imagination. Your brain doesn't know the difference between an imagined experience and a real one, so use this to your advantage. This should give you a feeling of euphoria and excitement, even if only temporarily.

It is helpful at this point to remember again your inner chimp, whose primary aim is to keep you safe from harm by encouraging you to keep things as they are, to avoid change at all costs. If yours tries to hijack your progress, politely remind it that you are just thinking through some options, not taking action, and there is nothing for it to get concerned about. There is a train of thought that you can simply 'exhaust' this hijacking by telling the chimp to 'Shut the f*** up' until it gives up the fight. My preferred option is not to fight fire with fire, but to talk the chimp down calmly until it gives in. Getting into a deeply relaxed state can help with this. I am no expert in meditation, but I have found that taking ten deep, slow breaths in through my nose, holding for five seconds and then slowly breathing out through my mouth for five seconds is incredibly effective.

Capturing your new reality

Once you have imagined your ideal life in all its detail, capture it by writing it down and keeping it somewhere accessible. When the going gets tough, return to it and remind yourself of why you are doing what you're doing and of the tremendous reward that is coming. Many of my clients write a letter to their future self, detailing everything they have envisaged, which helps cement their desired future in their mind.

One of the most common underlying symptoms of Imposter Syndrome (according to my own research of over 250 professionals) is a significant lack of feelings of fulfilment. This is linked to believing we are missing out and not living the life we wish we were living – the one that we'd require more self-confidence than we currently have to achieve. Once you start developing your vision of the future and the belief that you can achieve it, you will have a chance of making it your new reality. Imagine how much more fulfilled you'd be knowing that every choice you make from now on will take you one step closer to your vision.

Remember that the brain looks for threats, this makes it hard to see the potential rewards – unless you choose to do so. Actively creating an exciting and compelling vision of the future helps move your brain away from threat and toward reward.

Once you have this vision in your mind, you are ready to look for ways to make it a reality. Start by breaking down your vision into smaller milestones that are less overwhelming to contemplate and create a timeline for reaching them. In other words, turn your vision into a plan. This doesn't mean you have to have realised your entire vision by a certain date, but set goals that you can achieve within six months, a year and so on. A plan without a timeline will allow you to drift off and procrastinate. Hold yourself accountable but be realistic. Set yourself up to succeed. If you can find an accountability partner or a coaching group to join, this will help keep you on track and push you to achieve more, faster.

Positive vibes

The next task is to identify what new thoughts, feelings and beliefs about yourself you will need to rely on for this new future to become a reality.

EXERCISE: Creating new beliefs

To get into a positive cognitive state, one which will drive and reinforce positive thoughts, feelings and behaviours, ask yourself:

- What do I need to be thinking? (For example, 'I can do this'.)
- What do I need to be feeling? (For example, 'This is exciting'.)
- What do I need to believe about myself? (For example, 'I am a confident, capable professional'.)

Write down your answers. Together, these will form your new mantra, which you are going to repeat, over and over. It may take some time for you to believe it, but you can fake it until you make it. It doesn't always need to be all three on repeat, some people have just one that stops them in their tracks and gets them in the right frame of mind. What you are creating is a simple impactful and repeatable 'pattern interrupt' to break out of old ways of thinking, feeling and behaving when they occur.

The case study below is a great example of how creating and reinforcing new, positive beliefs can dramatically change your future outlook.

CASE STUDY: GENERATE

N came to me after having been made redundant, landing a new role and just a few months later finding himself out of work again. He felt worthless and unemployable, believing that his professional life was over.

We worked together for a few months and reached the third step of the EAGLE system, where he wrote down his new beliefs, his mantra:

- I am a valuable asset.
- I am confident that I can add value.
- I can and will make a positive impact, fast.

When N arrived at the interview for a senior leadership role, he was 'leaking' completely different vibes to those he had been just a few months earlier. He got the job, and when he starts his new role he will continue to rely on this new set of beliefs alongside his skills, and he will succeed. He is empowered and in control of his future, which makes him feel great.

Once you have done the hard work and created your mantra, you must memorise and use it regularly, which means several times a day. This is the only way it will change your life. Below are some examples of how my clients have managed this successfully.

- B landed on a key word that triggered her ability to be the empowered, strong, confident person she wanted to be. She had this word engraved on a ring she wore every day and could look at whenever she needed to. This worked particularly well in interviews or challenging meetings where her old self-limiting habits were most likely to re-appear.

- H had post-it notes everywhere with her mantra written on them. Wherever she looked, she was reminded of it, which kept her laser-focused on her plan. Whenever she felt that her commitment to change was waning, she would remind herself why she was doing it and the benefits and rewards she would gain. It wasn't long before amazing things started to happen, doors opened she didn't even know existed, which further fuelled her desire to keep going.

Visual reminders are powerful and help keep us on track. Whenever we see them, we subconsciously absorb their message, which strengthens the new beliefs we want to embed. You have decided to make this your new reality, so make sure you stick to it. Once you have embedded your mantra in your mind, you will need to remind yourself of it less often. You will have created a new neurological pathway – remember, the more you use it, the stronger it will become, so make sure you get a good return on the investment you've made by using it often.

Summary

- You have more control over your future than you might have realised.

- You can create new beliefs that are more helpful in moving you toward the life you want.

- New beliefs will lead to new outcomes.

- You are hardwired to look for threats, so you need to actively envision your possible future consciously and actively in all its glory to give your brain a chance of contemplating it as possible.

- Creating a vision of the future and working towards it will trigger feelings of reward and increased levels of fulfilment.

- Creating and repeating a mantra that encapsulates a new set of beliefs is essential to make your new way of thinking your reality.

- Beware of your inner chimp trying to hold you back and keep you stuck.

7
Step 4: Learn

You are now at Step 4 of the EAGLE system and will be glad to know that you have already done the most challenging part of the work required. It's now time to turn everything you have learnt into new habits that will make a positive mindset your new reality for good.

It is at this stage that people can easily get derailed, thinking 'I've got this'. Don't be fooled – changing the habits of a lifetime is not that simple. You will need to be super vigilant over the next few months as you put this step into practice. Take some time to review the earlier sections on change and remind yourself of how your brain may work against you as you implement your changes. In Part Three, we'll go into the process of change in more depth – watch out for the resistance and confusion stages, which can hold you back from the future you dream of.

As we have seen, changes or modifications in our behaviours and ways of 'being' or 'doing' are interpreted by the brain as a threat. As a result, your inner chimp will do all it can to take you back to the safety of old, familiar patterns of thinking, feeling and doing, even if these are harming you in the long term.

Practice

There are no shortcuts, no magic bullet for this part of the process. The only way to make sure that the new thoughts, feelings and behaviours you have generated in Step 3 become habitual and change your life, is to practise. The success of this step is all down to determination and resilience on your part. Skipping it can seriously impede your ability to successfully change your habits and overcome Imposter Syndrome.

When I tell my clients that the secret to engraining habits is practice, practice and more practice, they invariably imagine that this is yet another thing they must fit into an already jam-packed day. In fact, practice does not take any extra time at all; you will simply be using the time you used to spend procrastinating and doom-looping to engage in more helpful behaviours.

When you start (and I'll explain how in the following chapter), it may seem a little clunky and you may not feel that you are getting it right, but that doesn't matter. Just by doing something different and getting a different response, you will start to feel more empowered and confident. You are showing yourself that you can change outcomes even if they aren't the exact outcomes that you want yet.

Planning

To practise effectively, you first need to plan. 'Failing to plan is planning to fail', as the saying goes. If you don't set yourself specific goals for your new behaviours and actions, the chances of them happening will be reduced.

Think of the day ahead. What are you doing? Who will you see? What opportunities will you have to try out the new more confident you? You already know what triggers your old pattern of behaviours (refer to your examples from the exercise 'Finding the source' in Chapter 5 for a reminder). You do not need to avoid these situations; in fact, these are the opportunities you need to take advantage of. Your old trigger situations are your new playground, where you can practise your new skills.

Are you feeling excited and raring to go, or fearful? If you are fearful, this is your monkey brain, that inner chimp, trying to stop you from moving forward. Return to Steps 1 to 3 and remind yourself of why you are doing this. Once you feel calmer and back on track, identify a few simple opportunities to practise and keep pushing yourself to do a little more every day.

Capturing

When on a learning journey, it is easy to forget what has gone before. Most of us are inherently bad at taking time to look back for the good things that we have done as we hurtle forward through life. One of the reasons for this reluctance to reflect is that we don't like looking too closely at what we haven't done well and why this might have been, which can be quite unsettling. Even the thought of analysing our past efforts can initiate a fight-or-flight response and so we shy away from it.

Capturing requires resilience, self-leadership and emotional self-control. From a rational point of view, we know that there is no need to feel threatened, that we can overcome this unconscious avoidance tactic and consciously choose to look back and honestly assess our successes and identify development opportunities.

As children, we are encouraged to recognise what we have done well, but as soon as we head into employment the focus shifts to what we haven't done well. We're always looking for knowledge or skill gaps and trying to fill them, rather than celebrating what we're already great at. It is rare to find an organisation with a robust review process that inspires employees to look back for the right reasons, and to find leaders who know how to give useful developmental feedback that helps employees understand what they are doing well.

A review should be an opportunity to look back and feel proud of how far you have come as well as how things could be even better in the future. This is exactly what you will be doing now by capturing your growth. It is important to make capturing what you have done well and monitoring your progress a conscious, active process so that it can help move you away from threat and toward reward.

If you don't know what you have done well, you are missing a positive learning opportunity and so it will be harder to repeat it. If you don't learn from your mistakes, you will be unable to plan to do something differently next time, something that may change the outcome.

In Part Three, I will explain how to coach others for improved performance. But you can do this for yourself, too.

EXERCISE: Self-coaching

To 'capture' your progress so that you can use it for consistent improvement, first identify an example of an action (or actions) you decided to take. Then consider how this was different to how you would have behaved before you started developing your mindset to be more confident and resilient. Ask yourself:

- Why did you choose to do/say this? What was your purpose and desired outcome?
- How did you do/say this and what did you achieve?
- What did you do/say well? What are you proud of?
- What could you do differently or even better next time?
- When will you try this again?

Ask yourself these questions often to embed your new behaviours and make them permanent default choices. Be completely honest with yourself and your answers will provide you with real gold to work with.

Many of my clients find it helpful to capture three things they have done well and three things they felt they could have done better, on a daily basis. This doesn't need to be a formal session or take much time. You can do it while getting on with chores or exercising. It may feel strange to start with but, as with any habit, it will quickly become your norm once you start seeing the rewards you get from it.

Taking just a few minutes each day to reflect, review and self-coach will allow you to feel the joy of success and show you how to keep doing better. Your self-awareness will dramatically improve and, in turn, so will your emotional self-control, which has an impact on everything you do and how well you do it.

Step 4 is a learning and growth phase. You are not expected to get it right straight away or every time. Doing this in a less than perfect way is not failure. This is learning in action. Trying something different and looking for ways to improve has a totally different impact on your mindset than seeking to avoid failure, so think carefully about the way you frame what you are doing.

You may be disturbed by the idea that you might do something 'imperfectly', which may well be your excuse for not trying something new, for giving up and reverting to your old habits. Well, get comfortable with being uncomfortable, because the chance of this working 100% perfectly first time is super slim.

Daniel Priestley, co-founder and CEO of Dent Global and author of *Key Person of Influence*, talks about being 'directionally correct' rather than aiming for perfection.[31] The key thing is to head in the right direction; you can work on perfecting things as you get more confident and skilled in creating your unshakeable self-belief. Good enough *is* good enough and is likely to be another person's idea of great.

Acting and reacting

One thing I can guarantee is that, as you become more empowered and confident, others will respond to these changes. We have already seen how your feelings and actions impact others. We hope and assume that their responses will be positive, but what if the changes you are implementing are good for you but bother someone else? For example, what if a change means that another person can no longer treat you the way they were before? If a change in your life means that you will see less of your family because you need to travel more (as a result of a new role or a promotion), or that your family will need to move to another part of the country or even a different one altogether? Are they going to accept this easily?

They will have feelings and fears associated with changes that you make and will therefore need time to go through their own innate fear response. Meanwhile, it may seem that they are trying to block you, which can prevent you from moving ahead as their fears remind you of your own. If you allow this to happen and don't see it for what it is, you may start to believe that the change you were heading toward is not worth it. Your inner chimp will have a field day – 'I told you so' will be the theme of its mockery.

A common example that many (including myself) have experienced at work helps to illustrate the kind of reaction we can encounter when we start to use our improved confidence, self-worth and self-belief to take control of our future.

Imagine you are being bullied at work by a senior leader. You have decided that enough is enough and will no longer allow this behaviour to continue. As a result of your work in Steps 1 to 4 you feel stronger and ready to say what needs to be said to put this bully back in their box, so you do. What happens next? This person picks up on the fact that something has changed, which triggers their fight-or-flight response. They may push to keep you in the pattern of behaviour that they are used to and want to continue. They may get angry. Or they may go quiet and ignore you. It is unlikely that they will simply apologise and promise never to bully you again. They will want to put *you* back into the box you were in, as this makes them feel safe and in control.

The important thing to remember in situations like this is that their reaction is their response to a change that they are uncomfortable with and is not your problem, so you must not allow it to derail you – this is what their response is intended to do. Just notice the difference in their behaviour and recognise it for what it is.

You may need to do this several times before the other person's behaviour changes but if it doesn't, you will have to get help at a higher level from either an internal or external source (HR, coach, lawyer). Just make sure you get the support you need during this process so that you can keep standing strong.

It might help you to think of this as a dance. You and the person reacting to a change you have made used to dance to the beat of the same drum, round and round in a familiar routine. Now one of you has stepped away from the routine – to put on some new music or add different steps. Of course, your dance partner will be confused to start with and try to get you back into your previous rhythm, but if you persist and teach them the new dance, they must eventually either join in or stop dancing with you.

Once we understand and accept that we can control our own actions but not those of others, and see other people's negative responses for what they are, we can choose not to let this affect us, understand that this is a typical reaction to change and keep moving onward and upward without getting derailed.

Always remember why you are doing this, how it is going to change your life and what rewards it will bring. Remind yourself also how life felt before – you do not want to go back to that. The stronger your 'why', the easier this will be. This is why the first three steps of the process are so important.

It's not all doom and gloom. Making changes leads to incredibly empowering and positive outcomes and some people will react positively and welcome your new attitude, as the case study below shows.

CASE STUDY: LEARN

I was working with G, who was unhappy in his current senior leader role. The company had a toxic culture that had really sucked the joy of leadership out of him.

This affected his ability to lead his team effectively and started to negatively impact his relationships with family and friends.

First, we worked on his mindset, building confidence and resilience. The next thing was for G to go through a robust 360-degree leadership feedback process. He was nervous about doing this as he knew he wasn't being the leader he could be or that his team needed him to be – and hadn't been for some months.

The feedback he received had a profound effect on G. It was what he expected to hear but had been kidding himself wasn't a big problem: that he wasn't listening, he was miserable, never available and he wasn't developing or inspiring his team.

Seeing these comments in black and white shocked him out of his inertia and he decided to act and prove he wasn't the uncaring, disinterested leader he appeared to be. He wanted to be trusted, respected and challenged and, when it was time to go, he would leave a positive legacy. That wasn't going to be possible if he carried on as he was.

G chose three specific leadership behaviours to work on that would improve his ability to empathise, develop others and improve his emotional self-control. He chose whom to work with, what to do, when to do it and how to capture the impact.

His team responded positively and the desired results were instant. This was hugely rewarding for them and for G. He enjoyed spending time with them and had open, honest, frank and inspiring conversations, which he'd been missing. He remembered how it felt to be a real leader – and that he enjoyed it! Once this spark was reignited, he started to feel more fulfilled, more in control and no longer had the urgency to leave and his focus became on being the best leader he could be for his team.

Summary

- To change a habit, you need to teach your brain a new way of operating. This elicits a fear response, which you must recognise and manage.

- Practice is essential to behavioural change. If you don't practise, your progress will be slow.

- Capturing your success and development opportunities through self-coaching is a necessary part of the 'learn' step. It expedites your success through consistently reviewing what you have done well and how you could do even better.

- If you don't look back and see what you have achieved and how far you have come, your brain will be able to keep you in a state of fear, which will limit your progress.

- Others will respond to your changes and may try to derail you, as you make them uncomfortable. They are having their own fear response to change. Stick to your guns.

8
Step 5: Evolve

The EAGLE system is about evolution, not revolution. Both refer to change, but whereas revolution refers to a sudden and dramatic change, evolution describes a slower, more gradual process.

Please note that for the following to work for you, it is imperative that you have agreed up front what success looks like and have this documented, confirmed by your line manager and kept for reference during your probationary reviews. It is also worth sharing these objectives with your key stakeholders (allies), so they are fully aware of your aims.

The aim of the EAGLE system is to modify unhelpful behaviours slowly and steadily, not change who you are as a person. You will still be you – but a more effective, confident and resilient you. The behaviours we focused on in the earlier chapters were those generated by the negative, self-limiting thoughts and feelings that hold you back. These are now being swapped out for more helpful behaviours that move you closer to the success you now know is possible. Here, we want to make those changes stick. This requires you to start proving to yourself and others how incredible you are. The secret to convincing yourself of your own value is reinforcement.

Reinforcement

Reviewing what we have done well reinforces the idea that our choices and decisions were worth putting ourselves in 'danger' for. It teaches us that having new beliefs and trying new things or taking the hard path is not going to kill us and shifts the balance of fear of failure to excitement at the possibility of success.

If we don't do this regularly enough when attempting to change and learn new behaviours, our brains will keep looking for problems and stay in a high-alert threat state, which is the very thing that is holding us back from the explosion of opportunities that we are trying to open ourselves up to.

We need positive reinforcement but cannot rely on others to provide it for us. Which means we need to do it ourselves. The best way to reinforce positive behaviour is through rewards.

Rewards

Think of rewards you can give yourself when you achieve your goals. Choose something that will embed the joy of achieving. This will help to establish a new thought pattern in which there is more possible joy than possible threat with this new way of being.

Rewards should be personal and do not have to be momentous. Sometimes the smallest things can make us ridiculously happy. For example:

- Take an hour out to do something you love but rarely get time to do.
- Book a trip to the theatre, get a massage, go on a night out, or go shopping.
- Enjoy a fine bottle of wine.
- Book your next holiday or mini break.
- Start a book you've been wanting to read for months.

You might decide to do something once a day to say well done to yourself, or maybe once a week. It doesn't matter how or how often you reward yourself, just make it something that you do regularly and that you will enjoy, to send a signal to your inner critic that you have succeeded and are growing.

One of the biggest rewards is, of course, your end goal, the ultimate success you want to have as a result of this personal development journey – whether this is moving country, escaping the self-limiting beliefs that are keeping you 'small', leaving a job or getting a new one. But if you only ever focus on the success that will come with achieving the big, hairy, scary goals you set yourself, you put yourself at risk of feeling a failure, as the magnitude of fear associated with the end goal is far greater than with the intermediate goals. You also miss out on enjoying the journey as opposed to just enduring it.

Focus instead on the small stuff, the milestones along the way of the bigger journey. Think of the domino effect: each domino you knock down passes energy to the next domino in line, so that they keep falling. The momentum builds and eventually the domino at the end of the line is also knocked over.

To keep energised, we need rewards, or we can run out of steam. Even just thinking about the rewards signals to your brain that this change is a good thing, by making you feel happy. When we feel happy, we release dopamine (the 'happy hormone'); this dopamine rush is addictive – once you start feeling it, you will want more. Rewards also calm your emotional inner chimp right down and you will notice that its negative chatter becomes quieter.

Making allies

Creating new beliefs and managing self-limiting ones is particularly important when starting a new role (when allies are essential for your success), but also when going for an interview, at end-of-year reviews, returning after a period of absence, or any other time that requires you to be at your best. To create allies, you need to be in control of your mindset and manage what you are leaking.

For example, consider a scenario where you need to influence a key stakeholder. This person can determine the success that you have (or don't have), so getting them on your side from the word go is essential. Your job here is to build trust fast by demonstrating empathy and credibility. You will need to understand their goals and challenges, what it is they need to help them achieve those goals and overcome those challenges. You'll need to work out how you can help them and how you can work together to avoid potential roadblocks.

To start creating allies, you will need to:

- Come across authentically and with the intent to help

- Ask great questions and listen carefully to the answers

- Share what you know

- Ask how you can help them overcome their challenges and achieve their goals

Getting this wrong in the first few days or weeks of a new role and failing to create allies will adversely impact you, the organisation and the employees you are responsible for. The ripple effect damages everyone. It is hard to build high-trust relationships when your mindset is not at its peak, exposing you to a high risk of failure. I have worked with many leaders that were being slowed down and incurring costs due to a failure to make allies. No one wins in such an environment.

Sharing

Reinforcement is only part of the story. You also want to start sharing the good news, great results and a little of how it's been achieved, with others who need to hear it. These might be the people currently blocking you from reaching your destination as well as those who want to help you – your employer or clients. It's important that they know about your achievements, as they pay your bills and have the power to increase your income and opportunities for future success.

When working for someone in return for a wage or a fee, we assume that they will:

- Remember exactly what we are working on and why

- Know what we are doing to achieve the outcome and how

- Appreciate the results we have produced

- Link those to the value we add

All too often, though, this isn't the case. Your job may be your priority, but it isn't necessarily theirs. You've been hired precisely so that they don't have to worry about it. This means that if you don't consistently and appropriately share what you are doing and link this to the results that are being achieved, the person paying your wages will be left to make up their own story of how you are doing it. This leaves you vulnerable to misunderstanding and gives you less control over your future success. This is one of the big contributors that I see when onboarding has failed.

Unless you can clearly and consistently share the journey you are on and the results you are creating (or have been part of creating), they will have no idea how much effort you have put in, how well you have done your job or how you contributed to the results produced for them. If they cannot see it, appreciate it and understand it, how can they value what you bring to the table? You need to help them see exactly how brilliant you are and how this benefits them.

It is usually at this point that my clients begin to look uncomfortable, as they tend to equate sharing success with 'showing off'. Far from showing off, you will be sharing your success in an emotionally intelligent, non-egotistical way that inspires both you and the receiver.

There is an art to sharing without bragging. First, you need to stop focusing on what you want and feel and consider who would benefit from knowing about the incredible results you are achieving, and why. This is likely to be your line manager and anyone else who is benefitting from or impacted by the work you are producing.

Once you've decided who it is appropriate to share with, identify how they like to receive information. Communication style preferences, which we explored earlier and will do again in Part Three, are key to sharing any form of information effectively. You don't have to share absolutely everything; share the news and results that will help the receiver trust you, do their job better and achieve their goals. Share with the intention of helping the receiver see the benefit to them and their business; this is not about blowing your own trumpet or self-gratification, just an essential step in ensuring those you work with see you as a highly valuable member of the executive team. Reference the impact on the mission or vision of the organisation and the departmental vision and goals to validate the importance of your work and the impact it is having.

Don't just randomly bombard people with this information; plan what you are going to share and practise doing so. Keep it simple, clear and be prepared with details in case you're asked for them. If you're asked a question you can't answer through lack of preparation, your news will not be received in the way it is intended. Make sharing progress and achievements a regular and important part of your meetings with the relevant people and encourage others to do the same. Good news and good feeling spreads like wildfire; be the spark that ignites it.

After sharing, notice how your information has been received and consider if you need to change anything about your delivery next time to help it have even greater impact. You can even ask the receiver for feedback: was this information helpful to them? How will they use it to drive their business success? What else do they need to know or see from you? Finally, capture what you did, how you did it, how it made you feel, what it made you think about and what you could do even better next time so that you can reflect and review this important step of your journey.

Sharing good news in the right way will help with onboarding success, accelerate promotions and attract more responsibility, bigger bonuses, new business and more clients, because it will increase others' confidence and belief in what you can offer them. It also does something else that you need. Sharing what you have done well and how this contributes to the success of others and the organisation helps to embed the new positive self-belief pathways that you have been working on in the earlier steps of the EAGLE system.

The case study below is a real-life example of the difference sharing can make.

CASE STUDY: EVOLVE

C is a successful C-suite leader. He came to me after being made redundant because he felt as if he had been stripped of everything he knew to be true about himself and his future. He felt exposed and vulnerable.

C had since set himself up as a consultant and was earning a decent income, but he had much bigger dreams, which seemed a million miles away. Like many of us, he put his head down and plugged away, rarely looking up to see what was going on around him, how things could be even better and, most importantly, how he could share his success with those who needed to know about it.

We worked through the five-step EAGLE system and from the beginning it was clear how he felt about sharing his success and awesomeness with others: this was something only show-offs did. He did not see the difference between helping a client understand how he was adding value to them and blowing his own trumpet for personal gain.

The work we did unpicked many mistruths about what he was doing, why he was doing it and how he would ensure his vision of the future could become reality. One of the biggest lightbulb moments was around C's belief that success was financial – that if he managed to buy and build his own company and then sell it for £X amount, that was success.

I asked him to imagine life with £X and whether that was all he wanted – it turned out it wasn't. After a little more probing, C began to see that money was just a by-product of success and could focus on what success truly meant. For him, freedom, autonomy and flexibility were what would make him truly happy.

With this knowledge, it became clear that the majority of what he was doing did not serve his needs but was easy for him to do. This easy path was not going to take him anywhere near what he wanted to achieve in the next five years.

One of the milestones on the way to C's goal was believing in his own capability. Another was creating more space to think and start doing the stuff he needed to do to make his life goal a reality. This would mean earning more money in fewer hours each week. C could now see the need to share his success and results with the people who were paying his fees and found a way to do it that wasn't showy.

His clients' conscious confidence in him soared and they asked him to do more and more for them. This allowed C to drop the clients that were not paying as well and to say no to 'opportunities' that were just road blockers, enabling him to do more of what he enjoyed, earn more and work fewer hours. His income increased but, even better, he had time back in his day to start creating the vision for his future

> company – how he would fund it, who he would
> work with and employ to help him. His belief and
> desire to take his dream to the next level became so
> strong that it was starting to become his reality.
>
> This would not have happened as fast (if at all) if
> C had not diligently worked through all the steps
> of the EAGLE system; but the biggest changes
> occurred when he started sharing his success with
> those who needed to hear it.

You cannot capture and share your successes with others comfortably and in an inspiring way if you don't believe in yourself. Improving your self-belief and confidence comes from unpicking all the unhelpful thoughts, feelings and beliefs that are taking up space in your brain and visualising another possible truth. It requires being crystal clear about what you want to achieve in life and having a robust plan to get there – a plan that you stick to.

Once you start to see the true value you add and feel excited about the future you want, you can identify all the smoke screens blocking you from the life you want. You can also help others see this value, which will have a positive financial impact (more meaningful work, more clients, promotions, higher fees).

Getting results faster

The shorter the gap between starting to make changes in your thinking, feeling and behaviours and seeing improved business or professional results, the better.

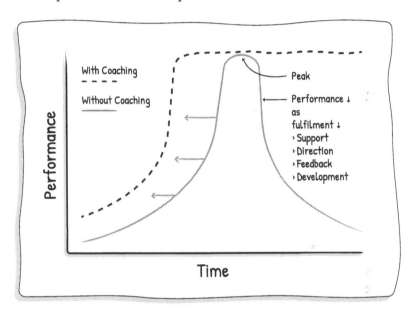

Time to peak performance with and without coaching

The figure above shows the difference in time taken to achieve your peak performance state (which allows you to achieve incredible results) when you are feeling confident in yourself and your abilities versus when you are fearing failure or preoccupied with what might go wrong. Your confidence not only impacts your ability to perform at your best, it also impacts the relationships you need to build and the time it takes for your organisation – especially if it's a new organisation for you – to recognise that you are an incredible asset.

With the right effort, dedication and support, it is possible to achieve significant goals – a promotion, for example – within just weeks. This is exactly what happened to one of my clients who onboarded into a new senior-level role and within six weeks had been promoted. She had managed to put her Imposter Syndrome to bed, just in time to start her new role, and is now firing on all cylinders, making a positive impact. This could be your reality if you choose to trust the process and do the work. All you need to do is try hard, believe in yourself and keep going.

You've now completed the EAGLE process. Welcome to your new life, one full of possibilities, happiness and even more success.

Summary

- The secret to making your changes stick is constant reinforcement.

- Sharing what you have achieved with others is also essential. This can feel uncomfortable, especially for those impacted by Imposter Syndrome but it is possible to do this without

feeling like a show-off when the intent to share
is right.

- Before you start sharing your success, make sure
  you have confirmed your criteria for success in
  writing.

- Choosing what to share for the right reasons is an
  essential part of your ability to create new, strong
  neurological pathways that cement your new
  unshakeable self-belief and related thinking and
  feeling – pathways you can travel down any time
  you choose.

- Sharing will highlight your achievements to
  those paying you and make them consciously
  aware of your value leaving far less open to
  misinterpretation.

PART THREE
LIMITLESS POSSIBILITIES

This book is intended to help leaders returning to work following redundancy overcome Imposter Syndrome and build the confidence to show up like the superstars that they are, feeling more fulfilled, in control and achieving even greater success. It will also be valuable for those starting in their first senior leader or executive level role and those returning to work post maternity/paternity or ill health as the related fears are similar.

In Part One we looked at identifying and managing Imposter Syndrome and in Part Two I shared with you my unique five-step EAGLE system for turning your vision of a successful and fulfilling future into your new reality. But for many in your position, this is not enough. Returning to work after redundancy presents special challenges and overcoming them requires knowledge and resilience. Ignoring these challenges or trying to mask them instead of accepting them and dealing with them puts you in a perilous position.

The same applies to those returning after maternity or ill health or starting new senior-level roles for the first time. Whichever 'camp' you are in, the following information will be of value to you now and in the future.

In this final part I will explain how you can further develop the mental resilience and 'leadership super-powers' which will keep your Imposter Syndrome at bay and ensure you stand out for all the right reasons. We will also look at the impact you can have on others through coaching and the difference between this, counselling and mentoring.

These skills and capabilities, in conjunction with your new unshakeable self-belief, will give you access to limitless possibilities – both at work and in your personal life. You will be more self-aware, make better decisions faster and with more confidence than ever before. You will handle difficult or tricky situations well and be treated with the respect you deserve.

Job opportunities will arise, promotions will be offered, contract rates will be set on your terms. Others will gravitate towards your positive energy, and you will inspire them to break through their own self-sabotaging behaviours. All of this is possible once you have banished Imposter Syndrome, taken control of your life and begun this transformational journey.

9
Mindset, Change And Mental Resilience

In Chapter 1 you learnt about the network of motorways in the brain (neurological pathways) and how these can be limiting and even harmful, and in Part Two I explained how you can replace them with more positive, helpful thoughts, feelings and beliefs using the five-step EAGLE system.

The sum of these thoughts and feelings is your 'mindset'. This drives your actions and has a strong bearing on the results you will achieve. The importance of a positive mindset on your ability to grow cannot be overstated. It is key to mental resilience, which determines your ability to bounce back from adversity, not live in a fairy-tale land of fluffy bunnies and unicorns!

In this chapter we'll look at the relationship between the three essential ingredients in the process of overcoming Imposter Syndrome – mindset, change and mental resilience – and how they can support you to enjoy a successful return to leadership.

A positive mindset

Earlier in the book we discussed fixed and growth mindsets. When you have a growth mindset, you thrive on challenge and see 'failure' as a springboard for growth and development rather than a way to describe yourself. Those suffering from Imposter Syndrome might deny their growth, operating instead with a set of fixed beliefs about themselves that hold them back. Having gone through the EAGLE five-step system, you now know how to understand, manage, and control those beliefs, if you choose to.

The characteristics of a positive mindset include hope, optimism, courage, realism and kindness. People with a positive mindset are less likely to give in to negativity, even in times of difficulty. They know that things can (and will) go wrong but focus on what they can do to make them go right as often as possible. To further develop a positive mindset that is geared toward growth, we need to be able to assess what we have control and influence over and therefore where to spend our time and energy resources that must be used wisely.

Those who focus on things they cannot control or influence at any level are 'burning fuel' on things that keep them unhappy and in a fearful state of mind. Their uncanny ability to see potential disaster, not possibility, around every corner holds them back and can be off-putting to those who want to look forward to the future. Remember, you are always leaking. Even if you think you are keeping negative, fear-based thoughts to yourself, they will be having an impact outside of you.

The case study below is a great example of how mindset informs thinking and, ultimately, results.

CASE STUDY: GROWTH MINDSET

K came to me after being made redundant twice, which she believed was the result of standing up for herself when things had become too much for her. She had been out of employment for over a year when we met but was keeping busy working as a consultant. The work we did on her confidence, perception of value and skills made a significant difference to her approach to job-seeking and her ability to inspire and build trust, and she soon landed the perfect role. Yet she still had concerns about the future, fearing that, even with her new-found beliefs and self-confidence, a redundancy could happen again.

This, of course, was entirely possible, if her beliefs about the reasons behind her redundancy were true and she found herself in a situation where she needed to stand up for herself. This would also mean that, if she chose to hold on to these beliefs when she started her new role, she would be reticent to speak up in meetings, share different or opposing views, say when things were getting too much for her, and feel uneasy saying no to things that were not her responsibility – all of this to avoid another redundancy.

Unfortunately, the result of these beliefs and associated behaviours (which were based on a fear of what could go wrong), could lead to a misconception in the brain of the receiver (eg K's line manager, new colleagues, team members) of how competent and valuable she was to the organisation. If this happened, it would create fear, tension would arise and trust in K would start to erode.

This posed a problem: if K continued to believe that standing up for herself and challenging the status quo led to her dismissal, there was a strong chance that the chain of events that had really caused this (which were different from K's perception), would remain unchallenged and be repeated, with the same unwanted result. We therefore needed to delve into the source of this misleading and potentially success-blocking belief to avoid this happening.

In her first role, K was told by her boss that she was a strong performer and had high potential. She was soon promoted to a senior global role in which she was overloaded with work; because she was still quite new, she didn't want to say no to anything. She wanted to feel needed and regarded as capable – a desire and need linked to childhood experiences, as K had grown up believing that her job was to please others and be useful by fixing problems.

As a result of consistent overload, K had to take three weeks off with stress and burnout. In this time, a new manager was appointed and his feelings about K were clear: she was clearly weak and of no value to him. Within a few months, even though she was back at work and, she thought, doing brilliantly, K was 'let go'. In her mind, K linked her dismissal to having been honest about her unbearable workload and standing up for herself by taking time out.

It was not K standing up for herself that had led to her dismissal; rather, her deeply engrained desire to be needed and fix others' problems had led to her ending up burned out. This is what led to the new boss's poor (and incorrect) judgement of her and her subsequent dismissal.

We needed to understand where the problem began to solve it and prevent it from happening again. There had been warning signs that dismissal was possible (the poor treatment, lack of care regarding her workload, time off with stress) and that it was time to move on, but K had been unable to see them, let alone respond to them, as she was too focused on trying to solve problems and prove her worth. This blurred her vision of what was going on around her. By accepting the situation she was in and allowing it to continue, those self-limiting beliefs embedded in childhood left her frozen and unable to leave. She was effectively a sitting duck.

The work we did together helped K make sense of the chain of events that really led to the redundancies and uncover the mistruths that would hold her back in the future. As a result of this work, she secured a job she wanted, on her terms. Not only that, when K started the new role, empowered, confident and believing in herself, she was promoted within weeks. Her skills hadn't changed but how she showed up and used them had.

The difference in K today is incredible. Her approach to challenges, both personal and professional, has transformed (she describes it as like living in a parallel universe), and her self-belief is still growing stronger every day. She has big plans for the future, which give her excitement and energy. All this in the space of twelve months.

The process of change

To experience the changes in mindset that I have described, you need to adapt your current behaviours and develop new ones. Knowing how your brain is working for or against you when a change occurs or is necessary means you can catch yourself self-sabotaging as it happens. This will help expedite acceptance of new and potentially scary situations and embrace the changes required to move forward.

Change is necessary and follows a predictable pattern. How long we take to move through each stage of change is what varies. Why should you care about this if you are returning to work, onboarding into a new role, or transitioning into another department or team? As you are settling in, everyone around you will be going through a change too. As I've already explained, change triggers a threat state that prevents us from performing at our peak and being the best version of ourselves. This is happening in the brains of our new colleagues too. This makes building trust harder and decision making poorer.

There are things you can do to manage the potentially precarious transition or onboarding period to help yourself settle in more effectively and get your new colleagues to accept you faster. Those who do this well will last longer in their role, enjoy it more and have greater success in a shorter space of time. This will give you even greater control over your future success.

To do this, you need to understand the process of change in a professional context, which consists of four stages. In this section, we'll explore these in depth so that you can recognise them and know what to do when you reach them.

Stage 1: Comfort

In this stage, before a change has occurred, we are comfortable with what we are doing and likely to be highly competent at it. Sooner or later, high achievers are likely to get bored and frustrated and look for other ways to satisfy their need for fulfilment. We are most productive when we are feeling inspired, excited and energised. A lack of fulfilment leads to a drop in productivity. This is not great for businesses that want to grow or teams that strive to perform to a high level. Some employees may want an easy, repeatable life that feels familiar and safe. They come in, do their job and no more. You may have heard these people described as quiet quitters. I won't go into detail about this phenomenon here, but it's worth noting that there are two main reasons employees quietly quit.

1. They have no desire for growth and want to do their job well, within the boundaries of their contract and then go home, on time, stress free.

2. They are unfulfilled, dissatisfied or unhappy and have switched off. They do what needs to be done (just about) but no more. This is fuelled by a feeling that can (and must) be addressed through effective and supportive leadership.

Consider the first group of employees; a common assumption amongst high achievers who see the world through their lens is that there's something wrong with these people. This isn't so. People like this are necessary in and valuable to an organisation. There are certain roles within all organisations where this attitude is perfectly acceptable – but not in a leadership position. You would have a problem if too many people in an organisation felt this way, as the company's ability to grow and remain competitive would be hampered, and those with a strong drive for growth would find this environment deeply dissatisfying and wouldn't stay for long.

Those with a high degree of Imposter Syndrome are interesting, as they can get stuck in Stage 1 (Comfort), appearing like a quiet quitter due to fear of the necessary change. This overrides their desire to move on, but it is still there.

To identify whether you are in Stage 1, ask yourself the following questions:

- Do your job-related tasks feel easy to accomplish?
- Does it take less time to complete your tasks than it used to?
- Are you getting bored and lacking fulfilment?
- Do you wish you had a new challenge to sink your teeth into?

It's not a bad thing to be in Stage 1. In fact, it is necessary to occasionally spend some time here to reboot, build your energy and avoid burnout. Consistent change for change's sake is exhausting and leads to lower productivity over time. But if you find yourself hanging out here for a long time, it is worth considering the reasons why.

Once your desire for change wins out, or change is imposed upon you, you leave your comfort zone and reach...

Stage 2: Resistance

At this stage, your brain senses a threat, and it really needs to know the 'why' to help it calm down. Change means difference and difference is dangerous. You will recognise this stage if you have ever wanted to make a change or do something that takes you out of your comfort zone but have been held back by the self-limiting beliefs and self-sabotaging practices associated with Imposter Syndrome.

Look out for comments or feelings like:

- 'I'm not going to do this.'

- 'I don't need to do this.'

- 'This is not for me.'

- 'It's pointless.'

- 'We don't need to do this.'

- 'This won't work.'

You may feel anger, frustration and disengagement; you may shut down and refuse to discuss the change. The impact of these feelings on your happiness, fulfilment and consequently your mental health is not to be underestimated. If you do not challenge them you can end up in a negative cognitive state that will bring others down with you.

Beware: not all resistance to change is unnecessary. Be prepared to dig deeper into the thoughts, feelings and beliefs behind any resistance before dismissing or giving in to it. This is much easier to do with confidence once you have mastered the EAGLE five-step system.

If you encounter resistance from others to a change you're making, you may feel your threat levels rise and be tempted to fight fire with fire. This will only make the situation worse. Understanding that this is a normal behavioural response to change is the start of learning how to respond effectively.

The first thing to do when dealing with your own resistance to change is to reduce tension. When tension is high, our ability to self-lead, self-manage and do the right thing is compromised. When in a threat state, we will not listen to reason; by reducing tension, we can open our ears and minds to what we need to hear and see to move forward.

Here are some tips on how to reduce tension caused by resistance to change:

- Notice and accept you are experiencing resistance to change.

- If possible, share your concerns with an empathetic listener, coach or mentor to help you identify the real reason for the resistance. Otherwise, ask yourself, what are you feeling and thinking? Where is this coming from? What is the real problem?

- Decide if the resistance is necessary and worth pursuing, or a fear response that is unfounded and needs to be managed not ignored.

Quick note to those of you leading teams. If you notice your team members are in this stage of change, it can be frustrating for you and for them. The following tips will help you resolve most situations effectively:

- Manage your own emotional response first (eg frustration).

- Be empathetic (show you want to understand and that you care).

- Seek to understand, not be understood.

- Listen and be sure you have heard what was said.

- Dig deeper – the truth of the problem is often hidden by many layers.

All the above suggestions will lower tension for every-one. This allows you to really listen and for them to share their fears and frustrations in a safe space. You can then move forward with whatever is necessary for the change to be possible.

Stage 3: Confusion

Once tension has been lowered and we are able to move on from resistance, the next stage is confusion.

This is rooted in the need to know the 'how' and the 'what' of the change. Here we are finding a way forward that solves the real problem revealed in the resistance stage. This may be a need for knowledge, support, training, or understanding of expected reward. These are the blocks we need to remove to embrace the change we are facing.

Be warned, it is common to swing back and forth between Stage 2 and 3 several times depending on the scale of the fear and/or confusion related to the change. The signs and symptoms of this stage are similar but different to those seen in resistance. Look out for:

- 'I really don't feel comfortable with this.'
  (As opposed to, 'This is not for me.')

- 'I don't understand how this will work.'
  (As opposed to, 'This won't work.')

- 'How are we supposed to achieve this?'
  (As opposed to, 'This is not possible.')

Again, your emotional response to the situation is critical. Listen carefully to what you are asking for or trying to do, and why. Emotional self-control and self-awareness are essential to effectively move yourself and others through the process of change.

When we recognise that these statements are a cry for help from a mind that is trying to buy into the change but doesn't understand how to do it or where to get help and support if required, not just a mind that is saying 'No', we can focus on finding a solution and moving on from confusion.

Not all problems have an easily accepted solution or a clear answer that can be given. There may be gaps – in knowledge, skills, or a lack of funding for the training required for a change to be executed effectively. In these cases, honesty is the best policy. Focus on what you can control, accept what you can't and find a way around the problem – make the situation the best it can be under the circumstances.

When people are lied to, or information is held back unnecessarily, this thwarts progress. It leaves people feeling unsafe, knowing something is 'off' which reinforces that threat state. If this stage is missed or mishandled, people are likely to do one of two things: look for reasons to leave and find somewhere where they feel more understood and cared for; or shut down so that productivity grinds to a halt. Quiet quitting or presenteeism are common in such situations. Both come at a cost that organisations would like to avoid but often do little to prevent.

To help ourselves and others move through confusion quickly and effectively, we need to increase the depth of our understanding of the situation to create a feeling of safety and security. Once confusion has been resolved and all concerned are ready to embrace the change, we reach…

Stage 4: Revitalisation

This is a great place to be. A person at this stage of change is excited about what they are doing, knows how to do it, why they are doing it, how and where to get help if it's needed. They accept the limits they are working within and feel great about the change.

The sort of behaviours we can observe that are associated with renewal are:

- High levels of energy and enthusiasm
- Going the extra mile when needed
- Finding ways to be creative to help yourself and others

When you are in a team of individuals who all feel like this, it is infectious. To keep this feeling alive, seek feedback, get or give yourself coaching and remember to celebrate success as it happens, to keep rewarding yourself for the great work you are doing. This will keep you far too busy to focus on what might go wrong.

We cannot rely on others to reward us (even if they should), but you have learnt how to do this for yourself (as well as give yourself feedback/coaching) in the EAGLE system. If you do get external rewards, these are a bonus. Feedback, coaching and reward all ensure commitment to change is maintained.

A note for leaders – be aware that productivity may decrease a little while everyone settles into the change. Things may feel clunky and weird to start with as you start to embed new ways of working or behaving. This may impact some things people previously did well, which can be frustrating, but give it time, accept that this is normal and stay on track by keeping the 'why' in mind. This is your north star.

Then that's it. The change is made.

Or is it? Once the shine has worn off and the new situation has become the norm, it too will start to feel familiar and comfortable and there will likely be a new change on the horizon. Then it's time to start the process all over again.

Putting up a battle whenever change occurs takes time and energy. Energy resources are finite, so finding ways to speed up the transition from Stage 1 to Stage 4 will help embed a new belief that not only is change possible, but it can be quick and not always stressful or hard.

Below is an example of a change process I coached one of my clients through.

CASE STUDY: A CHANGE PROCESS

F was the owner of a medium-sized organisation. He was doing well and wanted to achieve more, but the interventions he put in place were making little difference. This was because they were geared toward improving others rather than improving himself as a leader. The change needed to start with him.

F was blocking greater success for everyone. His employees were highly capable; they had just lost their mojo and were feeling unfulfilled and lacking motivation. After getting my feedback on how his behaviours and leadership style were impacting his team and the business's results, F simply refused to take the comments on board. He gave every excuse under the sun as to why his behaviour was not impacting the results. He was in Stage 2: Resistance.

I gave F some space and time to chill out and think. Then, during the next session we looked closely at what F was so averse to and triggered by. This uncovered that:

- He didn't like to be told what he was doing wrong, which was how he had chosen to interpret my feedback – his perception was his truth.

- He didn't know if he could make the business grow any other way (self-limiting belief).

Once F understood that the feedback was not an attack on him or his character, the perceived threat and his associated fear response started to subside.

We then turned our attention to his self-limiting belief that he couldn't lead any other way. F believed his brain could only work the way it did and the idea of changing the way he had always done things was a huge challenge.

He was in Stage 3: Confusion. I explained clearly what needed to be done and how it would be achievable with my support. He realised that the changes he could make to get the impact he wanted were not huge, that small tweaks would have a big impact.

After several weeks of trial and error, F began to see the difference these changes were making to his team's morale and their productivity levels. The greater the productivity, the better the results. This spurred him on to keep going and he swiftly moved into Stage 4: Revitalisation. There, he continued to hone his new skills and beliefs to achieve consistently great results. His team were more engaged and fulfilled and the business results improved rapidly.

Mental resilience

Mental resilience is the ability to handle change and ambiguity well, making us feel more in control of our lives and able to cope in times of stress. It also increases our ability to manage our emotions, which is essential when you are leading yourself (or others) through change.

Those who are more mentally resilient bounce back faster from adversity and it is a hugely helpful weapon in the fight against Imposter Syndrome. Yet it is something we seldom work on or even think about. In my experience, many people don't know what it is, how to improve it, and the potential gains, both personal and organisational, from doing so. I will answer these questions in the sections below.

What is it?

Some people are born mentally tough. They have a natural psychological edge that allows them to manage situations others find hard to cope with. Mentally tough people often take greater risks, are more likely to step out of their comfort zone and push their bodies to limits others couldn't contemplate. We see mental toughness in, for example, great athletes and those taking part in high-level competitive sports.

For high achievers, those leading teams and running organisations, their resilience will be severely tested on their way to the top, but the good news is we can all learn to increase our mental resilience and 'toughen up'.

How can I improve it?

The EAGLE system, though designed to help overcome Imposter Syndrome specifically, has value that extends far wider than this. It builds mental resilience and will change the way you view and engage with the world, while giving you coping strategies to use whenever your resilience is tested.

Mentally resilient people know what they can control and influence. They focus on these things, not those outside of their control. Being mentally resilient requires you to make wise use of your energy.

What are the potential gains?

Confidence is a key benefit of mental resilience. The more we recognise and use our skills, the more time we spend in a growth mindset, and the more willing we are to learn and evolve, the better we will be for ourselves and others. For leaders, this means they can create high-performance cultures where everyone thrives, which is always good for business.

There are mental and physical health benefits of mental resilience too. Those with better mental resilience are not only able to achieve more but also tend to have lower levels of ill health (and thus less absenteeism in the workplace). It has even been shown that resilient individuals have a better ten-year survival rate than non-resilient individuals.[32]

A recent review of the research on resilience suggested it leads to or contributes to many different positive health outcomes, including:

- More positive emotions and better control over negative emotions

- Fewer depressive symptoms

- Greater resistance to stress

- Improved immune system function

- Better ability to cope with stress, through enhanced problem solving and re-evaluation of stressors[33]

My own research and experience confirm that people who are mentally resilient are more likely to lead happier, healthier and more fulfilling lives with greater levels of success. Knowledge of how to build and maintain mental resilience will help you stay ahead of Imposter Syndrome and thrive in your return to a leadership position.

Summary

- Change is necessary and the process follows a familiar pattern, irrespective of the nature of the change.

- Change elicits a fear response that is innate and unconscious; we can bring these thoughts and feelings into our conscious mind and have more control over them, if we choose to.

- The four stages of change are: comfort, resistance, confusion and revitalisation.

- How long it takes you to move through the stages of change depends on several factors, including your ability to recognise and respond to the symptoms of each stage.

- When we understand change, how it impacts us and how to recognise what stage we're at, we can use effective interventions to expedite the change process in ourselves and others.

- Imposter Syndrome is due in part to self-limiting beliefs associated with fear of change. Understanding what the real fear is and where it is coming from is essential to move through the change process faster.

- Mentally tough and resilient people will cope better in times of change and ambiguity.

- Mental resilience can be improved with practice, with the help of the EAGLE system and by recognising what you can control/influence and focusing your time and energy there.

- Improving mental resilience will have a positive impact on your life, your health and your ability to lead and achieve.

10
The Leadership Superpowers

Taking control of Imposter Syndrome is important for anyone who is impacted by it, but particularly so for leaders, whose role it is to inspire a team and lead by example. Leaders are not immune to Imposter Syndrome and returning after a period of absence is a time when you may begin to question your ability, your knowledge, your relevance – all at a time when you want to be exuding confidence and getting buy-in from what might now be an unfamiliar team, showing them what a great leader you still are. The good news is that, armed with your new confidence and beliefs about yourself, you are in an ideal position to unleash your leadership superpowers.

Unfortunately, many leaders don't get the training and support they need to be good or great leaders, which is one of the reasons why organisations across the globe have so many problems with absenteeism, presenteeism and attrition rates. Being a leader is not something the majority naturally know how to do. It takes time, years of practice and plenty of 'failures' to be great at it. When leaders get it right, they save time, money and energy but, more importantly, the impact on the mental and physical health and wellbeing of all employees will be dramatically improved. This will allow leaders to leave a legacy they can be proud of. If you don't want to be the type of leader that others respect and want to work with or for, you probably aren't in the right job.

There are many ways for a leader to carry out their role more effectively and efficiently. From my experience, I have identified four key leadership 'superpowers'. Within these superpowers are an abundance of skills and tools that enable leaders to do and be better, such as giving feedback, coaching, listening, handling poor performance. All of these are essential for any leader who wants to perform at their peak and inspire others to do the same.

The four leadership superpowers we will focus on are:

1. Building trust through effective communication

2. Emotional intelligence

3. Working with the five human needs

4. Control and influence

In this chapter, I will look at each of these superpowers, which together will enable you to use your improved level of confidence and resilience to prevent yourself slipping back into old, negative behaviours, thoughts and feelings and to lead your team to achieve fantastic results.

Building trust through effective communication

Developing the ability to adapt your communication style to each person you interact with is a leadership superpower as it enables you to build trust. Where there is low or no trust, good, productive working relationships are hard to develop, which slows decision making, causes friction and costs the organisation money.[34] Creating high levels of trust quickly and maintaining this is key to success in *all* aspects of life.

Effective communication can help you win or lose trust. Successful people who want to be highly regarded and leave a positive legacy, rather than a trail of disaster, know how to communicate with all kinds of people. In Chapter 4 we looked at how to identify your own and others' preferred communication style. Here, we are concerned with how to adapt or modify your communication style to make another person feel more comfortable.

There are several tools that can help you to achieve better results by identifying and understanding how others like to communicate, such as Myers–Briggs, DISC, Insights Discovery, TTI Success Insights and Spotlight.[35] Whichever tool you use, the important things to remember are:

- You can adapt how you communicate at any time, if you want to.

- You aren't one-dimensional; your 'style' is simply a set of repeatable behaviours that help others identify your communication style preferences.

- No style is better than another; a variety of styles is important to aid diverse thought and innovation that leads to business growth.

Knowing this and applying it are two different things. The only way to effectively communicate in a specific, deliberate way is to consistently practise (every day) and make it a habit. Below are some top tips on becoming a master communicator:

- Know your own communication style and understand how you are perceived by others.

- Identify your communication strengths and what to watch out for when under pressure – in these situations you will have less emotional self-control and so be less versatile in your approach to others.

- Observe those around you and identify their behavioural and communication preferences and note the differences and similarities between you.

- When trying to build trust, minimise the differences between you by adjusting your communication style to be more aligned with the person you are communicating with.

Making small tweaks to one or two of your preferred behaviours is all that is required. The aim is not to change who you are.

You do not need to be versatile all the time. If you try to, you will soon run out of energy; it is counterproductive. You will also come across as disingenuous, a big trust killer. The only times to consider 'flexing' your communication style is when there is a problem that needs resolving and tension could be high, in establishing a new working relationship and most definitely during an interview and the first ninety days in a new job when you are building alliances and trust with others. When you do this with the right intent (to help others feel more comfortable so you can all achieve better outcomes, quickly) you will notice that conversations, even on tricky, contentious topics, become easier.

Emotional intelligence

Gone are the days where leading by rule was accepted, yet sadly it still exists and continues to have a negative impact on those working in such environments.

Too many senior leaders are appointed or promoted based on their IQ or sales results and not enough are given the training and support they need to become leaders in the true sense of the word – and organisations wonder why things don't run smoothly.

It has been proven time and time again that senior leaders who have higher levels of emotional intelligence (EI) get better results than those who have only a high IQ.[36] Most of us are not natural-born leaders and have to develop our emotional intelligence, which is the ability to identify and effectively manage our emotions and those of others. The more senior position you hold, the more important this ability becomes. Leadership with EI is about employing 'soft' skills such as the ability to inspire, guide and influence, as opposed to technical, task-related skills. These soft skills are a lot harder to acquire. Behavioural change, working against natural instincts, managing your threat response – your journey thus far should have shown you that these are some of the hardest of skills to master.

The four main EI competencies are:

1. Self-awareness

2. Self-management

3. Social awareness

4. Relationship management

Every leader and business owner will benefit from knowing what these are and how to demonstrate them. If you want to be great at what you do, they require re-visiting at regular intervals to check for progress and identify areas for development. Within each of these overarching competencies are various capabilities and specific behaviours. For example, social awareness consists of three aligned capabilities, one of which is empathy; the behaviours you can use to demonstrate empathy include showing an understanding of another person's perspective.

For the statisticians reading this, you will have worked out that there are ninety-two behaviours that characterise an emotionally intelligent leader.[37] Don't worry, you cannot be expected to demonstrate all of these, all of the time. You are human, after all. Aim to make improvements in one or two areas at a time to become the best leader you can be in the environment you are in. It's worth remembering that we can't all be great at everything. It would be unfair to expect that of yourself, so play to your strengths, develop new skills and minimise your areas for development. (I do not like the word weaknesses!)

Some of you will be moving into small, fast-growth organisations, some will be heading into turnaround situations, or something in between. You will therefore also need to be able to consider and adapt your leadership style to the needs and goals of the organisation and the people you are working with, while remaining authentic, human and empathetic.

Overall, there are six leadership styles that people fall into:

1. Visionary

2. Coaching

3. Affiliative

4. Democratic

5. Pace setting

6. Commanding

We tend to prefer one of these styles and stick to it, but this ensures we fall short of being the leader we could be. Emotionally intelligent leaders know which style to use when, and why. To be a great leader, you don't need to be perfect. You do need to understand yourself, manage your emotions, keep an open mind, focus on personal growth and development and care more (or at least as much) about the people you serve than yourself.

Now that you have done the work to take control of Imposter Syndrome and grow your confidence and self-awareness through the EAGLE five-step system, this will be a much easier task. Emotional intelligence is a leadership superpower because without it, our judgements and decisions can be biased and unhelpful; we see things only through our own lens and are oblivious to other possibilities. As a result, our behaviour may not only limit our potential to thrive and achieve but also make others feel uncomfortable and thus impact our working relationships, leading to higher rates of absenteeism, presenteeism and attrition.

The five human needs

Humans have certain needs that, if met, enable them to thrive and perform at their peak. Conversely, if these needs are not met, fear increases, fulfilment decreases so productivity drops and business results suffer. Yet these needs are rarely discussed in development conversations.

The five human needs that must be met to enable people to feel safe and prosper are:

1. To feel valued

2. To feel informed

3. To feel trusted

4. To feel connected

5. To be treated equally

The reason for high onboarding failure rates is often these needs being overlooked or ignored. Not understanding your needs and those of others could hugely hinder your return to leadership and your fight against Imposter Syndrome, so let's take a detailed look at each of them in turn.

How can you help others feel valued?

A leader who makes others feel valued will be providing regular, consistent feedback, coaching and recognition for a job well done. They will do this in a style that the receiver is comfortable with.

This checklist may be useful to help you assess how much you are currently doing to make those you lead feel valued:

- How often are you checking in with your employees one to one?

- What type of feedback and coaching are you providing?

- What type of recognition are you offering that is specific to the individual?

There are no set rules for how often you should check in with people on this, but you can ask people and agree how often you will meet, and you can notice when someone's productivity levels appear to be dropping. When this happens, you can safely assume that what you are doing is not enough.

If someone is new to an organisation or starting a new role within their existing organisation, it is wise to check in with them more frequently. Make sure you get to know them personally, find out what's important to them, what their aspirations and dreams are, then support them in this – be sure that they under-stand what they are doing, why they are doing it and what success looks like for them.

As a new senior employee, you should find this happen-ing for you too. So many new leaders are left to guess what needs to be done and what the priorities are. So it's no surprise that, when it comes to assessing the results of the probationary period, things are misaligned, and an onboarding failure appears to have occurred.

Part of setting yourself up for success in your new role requires you to be completely clear on what success looks like, how often you will be assessing your prog-ress, with whom and how during your probationary period. If this is undefined or woolly, you are heading into dangerous territory.

How can you help others feel informed?

It is essential to ensure that employees know where the company is heading, why and how, and what they can do to help this journey be a success. This requires:

- Having a clear and compelling company vision (and taking time to understand corresponding departmental visions that should be aligned)

- Making sure everyone is on board with the vision and inspired to achieve it (linking this to personal motivations is essential)

- Having clear, concise, emotionally connected goals (underpinned by the right behaviours) that you refer to in your regular feedback and coaching sessions

Keeping others informed is especially important in onboarding situations and times of change, but it is often missed or done so badly that it causes more problems than not doing it at all.

Of course, there are times when secrets need to be kept but this is not an excuse to say nothing at all. Simply explaining that a situation is developing is often enough to prevent rumours spreading and fear taking over. Above all, make sure that no one is given a preview of an upcoming change that is not allowed to be shared with the rest of the team. This looks like preferential treatment and causes tension. Saying nothing and hiding details when change is coming is simply not an option if you want your business to keep performing and produce great results.

How can you help others feel trusted?

Too many leaders adopt a default 'command and control' style (micromanaging), which stifles others' creativity and the incentive to improve current processes. There will, of course, be rules and guidelines for employees to work within, but we all need some free rein to explore, experiment and grow. Holding people back will make them feel untrusted and like they are not valuable; their sense of fulfilment will diminish and so too will their productivity.

To ensure that you get this right, first consider the person and the specific task they are performing – provide the right level of support and direction for them. Too much of either when they don't need it will be unhelpful and look like you are micromanaging, which erodes trust. Be careful also not to give too little support and direction when the person needs it, as this leaves the employee feeling vulnerable and exposed. These feelings are not conducive to high performance.

Second, do not assume that experience means ability, especially not in all tasks an individual is performing. Again, consider the person you are leading and the specific task they are working on. It is easy to make the mistake of assuming that if someone is new to a role, they have no experience or ability in any aspect of that role. They will bring many transferable skills with them and may not require much help from you. Not all tasks in the job description will require the same skill and experience level and so will require a different approach from you as a leader. Finally, learn more about the different leadership styles you could employ in different circumstances and with different people, to be a more effective leader.

All of this will not only help those you lead to feel trusted and valued, it will also give you time in your day to do what *you* need to do. Most leaders would welcome a few extra hours in their week.

How can you help others feel connected?

Helping others feel connected has become tougher with the recent increase in remote working, but this should not be an excuse for failing to make the effort to do so. On the contrary, it should make it even more important.

Everything I have mentioned above is relevant to building connectedness, but in addition, consider whether you're having regular one-to-ones with all your team members that include a personal and empathetic conversation about how they are feeling and what they are thinking. Do they trust and like you enough to be having these conversations? How do you know? Regular team check-ins, preferably face to face, with a clear purpose – to move the business forward, solve problems, share ideas and have some fun – are essential. They should ideally take place at least once a quarter.

If you are trusted as a leader, you will be able to connect far better than if there is low or no trust between you and your team members, which inevitably leads to a disconnect. Trust is developed through demonstrating empathy and credibility.

How can you help others feel they are being treated equally?

If you are doing all of the above to improve feelings of being valued, informed, trusted and connected, it is likely that your employees/team will feel that they are being treated equally, too. But there's more to it than that.

We are all biased in our way of thinking, being and behaving, which can lead to us having misconceptions or making unfair judgements about others. We are also hardwired to look for familiarity, as familiarity means safety. Anyone who is unlike us in some way can prompt a fear response that, if not acknowledged, understood and consciously managed, can lead to us to treat people inequitably.

To ensure that you are leading everyone equally and avoid causing perceptions of unfairness or favouritism, you should:

- Improve your self-awareness and emotional self-control to help you distinguish between truth and a perception based on your (potentially untrue) beliefs

- Ensure that you provide fair rewards based on objective feedback grounded in facts, not feelings

- Encourage everyone to contribute equally to meetings and make space for everyone to add value in a way they are comfortable with

- Provide an opportunity for relevant and inspiring development and growth to all – not just those identified as the 'top talent'

Meeting your own as well as others' needs

To reiterate, the five human needs are to feel valued, informed, trusted, connected and that we are being treated equally. You may have an instinctive pull to one or more of them over others or find it hard to assess which are more important to people in a particular situation. It's not always obvious.

Don't worry if you are unsure of your own needs or those of others sometimes, your aim is to meet the five needs as often as you can, not all the time. Aim to do it better than you were before and to keep improving.

If you are interested in understanding which of the five needs is more important to you (I'll let you into a secret – all five matter equally to me), consider times when you felt that your sense of fulfilment and performance dipped and ask yourself:

- What happened?
- Why did it bother me?
- Which of the five needs was/were not being met?
- Does a failure to meet these needs show up in other examples too?

The more conscious you are of the five needs and how to meet them, for yourself and others, the more natural it will become and the less energy it will take, leaving you more to spend on learning, improving and becoming an outstanding leader. Having their human needs met makes people feel safe. When people feel safe, they are more likely to look for the benefits and rewards of what they are doing, not the risks and dangers. This is a positive state to be in, and feelings of fulfilment and performance follow.

Finally, if you are not getting what you need to meet *your* needs, do not allow this to continue, as it will impact your ability to thrive and achieve what you are truly capable of. Do what *you* can to get what you need, how you need it, when you need it – which brings us to the next section.

Control and influence

There is much in the world that we can do little about: the traffic, the weather, war, pandemics, the football results... Spending time and energy worrying about such things is not only pointless, but also means you are losing out on something else that you can impact.

There is a big difference, though, between what is truly out of your control and what you have decided is out of your control. If you lack self-awareness and self-belief, it's easy to confuse the two. Leaders who can quickly and accurately identify what they can and can't control or influence and who focus only on the former are more effective than those who can't.

Control

In a business context, there is a tendency to get bogged down by things that we have no control or influence over. An example of this, which I hear year after year, is the complaint: 'The company keeps raising my teams' sales targets and they're impossible to achieve.' All sales-based organisations need to keep growing or they will fail, which means that sales targets will increase. This is non-negotiable and out of your control, yet the amount of time people spend worrying about it is unbelievable. I used to do this myself, so I know exactly how it feels.

What is the real problem? I've found that it is often simply the fear of having to keep proving yourself again and again, knowing that this will be hard work. What you can control in this situation is your reaction to it. Many believe that their thoughts, feelings, mood, behaviour, reactions, attitudes, etc are not within their control. They don't understand that, although these things may happen automatically, instinctively or unconsciously as an innate response to an external event, as explained in Part Two we can, if we want to, choose an alternative response. Choosing not to believe this is, of course, an option, but how will it help you?

Influence

Your reaction to a situation that is out of your control might not change it, but it can influence the outcome. Sticking with the sales target example, as a leader, the way you react to the new target will heavily influence your team's thoughts and beliefs about it. If you decide that it is impossible or unfair, you will leak this negativity to your team, leading to sub-optimal results (at least in the short term). Choosing instead to manage your emotions and leak a positive, can-do attitude will have a beneficial effect. It's important to be honest about your feelings here but in a way that does not elicit a threat response in others. We can't hide what we are feeling and thinking; it leaks out of us unconsciously. You can acknowledge that meeting the goal will be a challenge but then look at how you have achieved a stretch target in the past and plan how you will make this one attainable too.

Let's take another example. If you are starting a new role, or in a new organisation and you meet the key stakeholders, who could potentially make or break your probationary period, you have a choice. You can either panic and stress about failing (where you will leak fear), or you can dig into your inner confidence and resilience and show them why you are exactly the person to invest their time in and support. Put yourself in the position of the stakeholders and imagine the difference between meeting someone full of excitement, possibility, self-belief and confidence (but no ego) and someone leaking fear and self-doubt. Which mindset will lead to a desirable outcome?

To take a final example, consider a senior leader who is being bullied by the CEO. Instead of leaving the company, they choose to stay. The bullying keeps happening and they feel more powerless by the day. They tell themselves there is nothing they can do; the situation is out of their control. They can't control the CEO, but they do have influence in this situation. They are choosing not to exercise it because they fear negative repercussions. This fear is driving their decision making and holding them back from what they need to do, which is to stand up to the bully and refuse to let the situation continue.

Summary

- Taking control of Imposter Syndrome helps you focus on what you can control and influence. This frees up time and energy previously wasted on fear and worry, which you can redirect toward being a great leader and driving progress and improved business results.

- Being able to communicate in a way that others respond to engenders trust, which optimises performance.

- The four leadership superpowers are: building trust through effective communication; emotional intelligence; meeting the five human needs; and knowing what is within your control or influence.

- Developing and demonstrating self-awareness and self-control can help to defuse stressful situations and facilitates change.

- Knowing what all humans need to thrive is necessary to ensure you and your team members feel valued, informed, trusted, connected and fairly treated.

- When we feel that our human needs aren't being met, we feel under threat, then our ability to perform is reduced; if this is prolonged, it can lead to increased levels of attrition, absenteeism or presenteeism, all of which come at cost to the business as well as the individual.

- Learning how to meet the needs of your team will lead to greatly improved levels of fulfilment, which in turn leads to higher levels of performance and better business results.

- Knowing what is and isn't within your control or sphere of influence enables you to focus your (limited) energy resources in a productive way.

- Even if you have no control over something, you may have influence over it; use that influence wisely.

- You have more control than you think. You may feel powerless, that things are out of your control, but simply reminding yourself of what you can control and influence will help you make empowering choices.

11

Improving Performance
For Better Business Results

Businesses are always looking at maximising return on investment. One of the biggest and most important investments a business makes is its employees, yet many businesses don't value this asset enough.

As we have seen, those impacted by Imposter Syndrome will benefit hugely from developing their self-confidence and building mental resilience and a positive mindset. This allows more active contribution, more creativity, better problem solving, more fulfilment, more calculated risk taking, inspiration, happiness and so much more. All of this impacts the success of the business through a corresponding increase in productivity and a reduction in absenteeism, presenteeism and attrition. Even a marginal gain for each individual, when multiplied by the number of employees in an organisation, can represent a significant gain for the business as a whole – which is why identifying and challenging Imposter Syndrome should be taken seriously by every business.

Identifying signs of Imposter Syndrome in others

The first thing to note is that it is not necessarily the leader's fault that an employee is struggling with low self-esteem or a lack of self-belief. Recognising that it is a problem for one of their team can make leaders feel guilty, but it may be nothing to do with them at all. It could be because of the culture in the organisation (for example one of low trust, low emotional intelligence) or, as we learnt in the first part of this book, the self-limiting beliefs may have been there for many years and would be manifesting for that individual at work irrespective of their environment.

We have seen that it is not easy to recognise our own level of Imposter Syndrome; it can be even harder to identify this in others, as they may be doing their utmost to disguise it. Return to the five levels of Imposter Syndrome given in Part One to help you and be careful not to mistake behavioural preferences such as introversion for Imposter Syndrome.

Here are a few clues to look out for that are common in those affected by Imposter Syndrome Levels 1 and 2 (High and Humble+):

- Consistently high achievers / overachievers working far too many hours

- Those who appear highly competent and yet (if you look and listen carefully) show a lack of confidence or self-esteem through, for example, self-deprecation, and avoiding extra responsibility / promotions

- Perfectionism

- Those who take a backseat in meetings and discussions but are not known for typical introverted behaviours in other settings

- Those who try to be something / someone they are not to fit in

- Those who are uncomfortable around senior leaders

- Those who downplay their accomplishments and contributions

- Slow decision making or avoidance of decision making

- Avoiding feedback – giving and receiving

For those residing at Levels 4 and 5 (overconfidence and extreme overconfidence) it is harder to pinpoint the cause of their behaviour without an extremely high level of trust and a willingness on their part to share and learn. You may find they push back, deflect the conversation away from their behaviour and make it hard for you to help them. Sometimes it's easier for a trusted third party to support this work but again, it will only work if the individual is open to it.

Whatever level you're dealing with, look for clusters of clues and remember that even the most extrovert of people can have Imposter Syndrome, they may just disguise it better.

Below is an example that may help you recognise the signs of Imposter Syndrome in a colleague.

CASE STUDY: SPOTTING IMPOSTER SYNDROME

D was a successful senior sales leader. He was outwardly strong-minded, confident and competent in his role.

Most people would have had absolutely no idea that he was suffering terribly with intense self-limiting beliefs, but while working with him we uncovered that he:

- Lacked confidence when talking to more senior leaders
- Did not say what he wanted to in leadership meetings

- Did what was expected of him and followed the crowd rather than stick his neck out and be shot down (which had happened too many times before)
- Was not fulfilled and desperately wanted to leave, yet worked ridiculously long hours, sometimes sending emails or messages in the early hours of the morning or while on holiday, to prove he was vital to the organisation
- Chose to stay and put up with it because he believed he was a fraud and would not get another job at the same level/salary elsewhere
- Was unhappy and withdrawn – and no one had noticed

Do you recognise any of these traits in your team members, or maybe in yourself?

Often, they can only be identified by looking and listening attentively, by hearing what isn't being said and digging deeper, by having regular check-ins, by asking about personal aspirations, by building trust through adopting an appropriate communication style, by showing that you want to help. All of this takes emotional intelligence.

How to help

Now that you know what to look out for and can distinguish between symptoms or signs of Imposter Syndrome and behavioural preferences, the next step is to get the person to recognise and acknowledge that they may be experiencing a level of Imposter Syndrome and it could be blocking them from what they really want and deserve. If you have a high level of trust with this person and they want your help and support, you could invite them to take the Impostometer test at https://impostersyndromelevel.scoreapp.com. Better still, if they are open to sharing the results with you, then you can either coach them through the EAGLE five-step system or find a coach who specialises in this area to work with them on your behalf.

If you are going to coach others around mindset or any other performance-related skills, the best way to ensure that your own learning becomes embedded, repeatable and part of your leadership excellence toolkit is to practise and ask for regular, focused feedback on your own progress.

Few of us enjoy receiving feedback on how we are doing. If it is given badly and with the wrong intent, it triggers a threat response. Knowing how to give feedback and doing it regularly (as well as receiving it) must be part of your day, every day, if you want to develop yourself as a great leader and help to create a highly fulfilling, high-performance culture.

Giving feedback

The most important thing to remember when giving feedback is that the intent behind it matters hugely.

If your intent is to listen and understand, this will drive different behaviours to an intent of 'telling' and 'solving'.

Observational feedback should be:

- Clear and positive: 'I'd like to talk to you today about X and see how I can help you or support you to do Y...'

- Based on facts, not judgements: 'I saw/heard/ noticed X. Tell me what was going on for you at that moment...'

- Helpful, future-focused and developmental: 'What will happen if we do X...? What will happen if we don't do X...?'

- Regular and consistent: 'Last time, we talked about X and you did Y. Tell me how that went...'

Provide feedback on what has gone well and what could go even better, remind others why you are doing this (to help them grow), and make it part of what you do each day. Growth is key; small steps can lead to huge strides in the future. Be warned, though, most people have an immediate fear response when feedback is offered. This is especially true for those with Imposter Syndrome who are waiting to be told how rubbish they are. This may be due to a negative past experience of receiving feedback, which might have been done badly and/or with the wrong intent. Many of us also remember that the only feedback we were given as kids was when we were in trouble. It's therefore no surprise that we have a strong negative feeling towards it.

This is why it's so important that feedback never be negative, even if the person has done something wrong or you are helping them exit the business. The intent should always be to help the person develop and grow, to learn and be better in the future.

Give feedback well and you will see the difference it makes, not only to the person receiving it, but also to your own world. What is essential is that your employees get the help they need, in the way they need it. If you are not able to provide it yourself, don't hesitate to look outside for that help and learn how.

Coaching

Coaching and feedback are not the same thing, although you may share feedback as part of a coaching process. Coaching is not telling others what to do or teaching them your way of doing things. Coaching is helping others understand what they do, why they do it, how they do it, what they are doing well and what they could do even better.

Here are my ten top tips for coaching, based on my experience of working with leaders:

1. Keep an open mind and avoid making assumptions, don't let your own experiences sway you. Emotional self-control and self-awareness are key.

2. Ask open questions and be prepared to share your experiences if need be – but this is about them, not you, so don't take over.

3. Give people time to answer and show that you are actively listening.

4. Go digging – initial questions often elicit surface-level answers; dig down to the truth, which is often a few layers deep. Prompting, 'Tell me more about that,' is a great way to discover more.

5. Empathise, don't sympathise – showing that you care, that you understand and aren't judging is vital to keep tension low and trust high. Simply sympathising and agreeing with the coachee is unhelpful; your job is not to solve their problems for them but to help them do this for themselves by getting a clear picture of what the real problem is and its causes.

6. Don't dismiss the person's problems – for example, if someone tells you they have Imposter Syndrome (or symptoms of it), telling them not to be daft and that they are great will not help. Ignoring a problem and hoping it will go away won't help anyone.

7. Don't write people off because they are different from you. You will be somewhat biased in favour of likeminded souls, but to have a high-performing team, you need different people with different approaches.

8. Communicate in a way the other person feels comfortable with.

9. End the session with a plan that they decide on and an agreed date to check back in on progress.

10. Follow up and catch people doing things well so that you can always be coaching. This creates a coaching environment that is valued, not feared.

Counselling and mentoring

Not everyone with Imposter Syndrome is coachable and you must be careful not to try to coach people who need a different type of support. This book is not aimed at helping you identify who these people are and what they need, but you should be aware that if your best efforts to coach someone aren't working and they are clearly stuck in old patterns of behaviour, counselling may be something worth exploring.

Both coaching and counselling are incredibly powerful tools (as I know from experience, having spent many hours on the receiving end of both at different stages in my life), but it is important to be clear about the difference between them and the purpose of each, so you know which to reach for.

Coaches assess what is happening with someone, uncover the reasons for this and help them make sense of those reasons and the impact of what's happening on them. They will then move on to what the person wants, encourage and support them in working to achieve this and keeping them accountable for their actions so they get the desired results faster.

A counsellor, in contrast, will dig deep into the past and re-live and revisit pains and problems until the person fully understands where they have come from and what impact they have had and may continue to have. They will identify deep-rooted triggers that may not be obvious without this level of introspection.

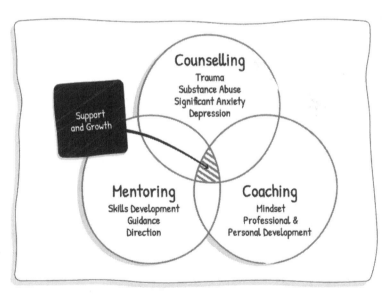

Coaching, mentoring and counselling

Another method of helping others grow is mentoring. Mentors are subject-matter experts who teach others the things they need to know to do their job better. Often, people call themselves coaches when they are in fact mentors, so it is necessary to be clear on the distinction. To clarify:

- Coaching is for successful, ambitious people who have a growth mindset and want to achieve more in less time.

- Counselling is for those who are struggling with the past, which is stopping them from moving forward.

- Mentoring is for skills transfer.

Summary

- People are an organisation's greatest asset and will provide a return on investment if their needs are understood and met.

- Organisations with a strong coaching culture and a focus on positive development achieve consistently better results than those that don't.

- Identifying whether people are being impacted by Imposter Syndrome is not always easy, but the effort will pay dividends.

- Regular, constructive feedback is essential for optimal wellbeing, fulfilment and performance.

- Coaching is a skill that all leaders who want to do a great job must acquire and can benefit you as well as the coachee.

- Not everyone will benefit from coaching alone; some may require counselling and / or mentoring.

- Identifying a person's needs is not always easy.

Conclusion

I began this book with a discussion of Imposter Syndrome – what it is, why those who have been made redundant or who are in their first senior role can be impacted by it, how to identify it and the effect it can have on you, the organisation you work for and many other areas of your life. I then discussed how to manage and control it, using the EAGLE five-step process. I showed you that it is not easy to recognise and change patterns of behaviour that you have embedded over many years – that it will take time, but that diligence and perseverance will pay off in ways you may never have expected. Finally, I pointed to the endless possibilities that managing Imposter Syndrome and taking control of your life can open up for your future.

The important thing to remember is that Imposter Syndrome does not reflect your capability and, once you have it under control, you will be able to perform at your peak more regularly and produce better results, for longer. You will be released from the shackles that held you back, allowing you to head full throttle into the future with new determination and clarity.

When I explain to my clients that their self-limiting beliefs and self-sabotaging behaviours don't have to be part of their lives any longer, I can see the relief on their faces as they start to imagine their lives without Imposter Syndrome being in charge, without anything holding them back from achieving their dreams.

Sometimes we have no control over our current circumstances, but we always have choices and so can change our future. Whatever it is you want, you can start working to make this your reality. You are capable of so much more than you realise; it's just a matter of figuring out how and being open to help if you need it.

Hopefully, you are no longer reading this thinking, 'Yes, but...' You should now know that this is your brain trying to keep you stuck in old, familiar patterns of behaviour, denying that you have control over what happens to you – classic self-sabotage. You also know now that this is normal and there is no need to panic.

You know that if things are bothering you or you are feeling frustrated with yourself, your behaviour towards others changes as your emotional self-control reduces. You are not as focused on doing your job or fulfilling your role as you could be. This means that you will not get the results you could have achieved, which has implications for the business and for you: if this is consistent over time, you may get overlooked for promotions, be in line when redundancies are on the cards, feel unable to ask for the rate you deserve and so on.

You understand that your brain is at the centre of your Imposter Syndrome mindset. Every experience you have ever had is held in this super-computer, which applies a filter to how you perceive the world and guides your decisions. Plenty of the beliefs that underlie your behaviours are created to help you make sense of the world around you and what's happening in your life in a way you can rationalise. These beliefs are often untrue, so make you more conservative, resistant to change and happy to accept the status quo.

We can get stuck in our tracks due to fear of the unfamiliar, the unknown, the new – fear of any kind of change. We can also fear what we will find in this unfamiliar new world, knowing that once we've found it, we will have to choose what to do about it, which is likely to take us away from our comfortable, familiar patterns of behaviour. You and I may know, rationally, that this 'stick as you are' option leads to less happiness, fulfilment and success, but still, we will resist change.

Fear of change and fear of difference are the main things that hold people back but what is there to fear, really? Ask yourself:

- What will happen if I make a change?

- What will happen if I don't?

- What is the worst that could happen?

In my role as a global executive coach, I teach a wide range of professional development and leadership skills, in both group coaching development programmes and one to one. When I introduce leaders to the information, skills, tools and techniques outlined in this book, the comment I hear most often is: 'I wish I'd known about this when I first started leading teams.' I hope you too have found them useful and that they will help you, and those you lead, to overcome any level of Imposter Syndrome you may be experiencing and move forwards into a bright and successful future – the sky is the limit.

Next steps

I have devised a simple test that will help you understand which signs of Imposter Syndrome you are showing and to what extent this is impacting you. You can take the test – 'Do I have Imposter Syndrome?' – at https://impostersyndromelevel.scoreapp.com.

If you'd like to discuss how EMR Consulting Ltd can support you, your team or your business, get in touch at www.emr-consulting.co.uk/contact.

Notes

1 J-M Sabel, 'Why more than 50% of new hires fail' (HireVue, 14 April 2017), www.hirevue.com/blog/hiring/why-50-percent-of-new-hires-fail, accessed December 2022

2 A Bryant, 'Corner office: Good CEOs are insecure (and know it)', *New York Times* (9 October 2010), www.nytimes.com/2010/10/10/business/10corner.html?_r=1, accessed December 2022

3 J Langford and PR Clance, 'The Impostor Phenomenon: Recent research findings regarding dynamics, personality and family patterns and their implications for treatment', *Psychotherapy: Theory, research, practice, training*, 30/3 (1993), pp495–501, https://psycnet.apa.org/record/1994-17499-001, accessed October 2022

4 Y Wang, K Hunt, I Nazareth et al, 'Do men consult less than women? An analysis of routinely collected UK general practice data', *BMJ Open*, 3/8 (2013), https://doi.org/10.1136/bmjopen-2013-003320, accessed October 2022

5 J Cafasso, 'What is synaptic pruning?' (Healthline, 18 September 2018), www.healthline.com/health/synaptic-pruning, accessed December 2022

6   K Armstrong, '"I feel your pain": The neuroscience
    of empathy' (APS, 29 December 2017), www.
    psychologicalscience.org/observer
    /neuroscience-empathy, accessed December 2022

7   E Jaffe, 'Mirror Neurons: How we reflect on behavior'
    (Association for Psychological Science, 2007), www.
    psychologicalscience.org/observer
    /mirror-neurons-how-we-reflect-on-behavior, accessed
    October 2022

8   T van Schneider, 'If you want it, you might get it: The
    reticular activating system explained', *Medium* (22 June
    2017), https://medium.com/desk-of-van-schneider/
    if-you-want-it-you-might-get-it-the-reticular-activating-
    system-explained-761b6ac14e53, accessed October 2022

9   C Dweck, 'What having a "growth mindset" actually
    means', *Harvard Business Review* (13 January 2016), https://
    hbr.org/2016/01/what-having-a-growth-mindset-actually-
    means, accessed October 2022

10 T Hines, 'Anatomy of the brain' (Mayfield, April 2018),
    https://mayfieldclinic.com/pe-anatbrain.htm, accessed
    December 2022

11 S Peters, *The Chimp Paradox: The mind management
    programme to help you achieve success, confidence and happiness*
    (Vermillion, 2012)

12 'Brain anatomy and how the brain works' (Johns Hopkins
    Medicine, no date), www.hopkinsmedicine.org/health/
    conditions-and-diseases/anatomy-of-the-brain, accessed
    December 2022

13 'Fight or flight response' (Psychology Tools, no date), www.
    psychologytools.com/resource/fight-or-flight-response,
    accessed November 2022

14 M Lewis, 'Why we're hardwired to hate uncertainty',
    The Guardian (4 April 2016), www.theguardian.com/
    commentisfree/2016/apr/04/uncertainty-stressful-
    research-neuroscience, accessed October 2022

15 'Imposter Syndrome: The secret fears of high achievers'
    (Instant Offices, no date), www.instantoffices.com/blog/
    featured/what-is-imposter-syndrome-at-work, accessed
    December 2022; 'Coping with redundancy during the
    pandemic' (Mind, no date), accessed December 2022

16　J Sakulku, 'The Impostor Phenomenon', *International Journal of Behavioural Science*, 6/1 (2011), pp75–97, https://so06.tci-thaijo.org/index.php/IJBS/article/view/521

17　D Tilo, '90% of female employees suffer from Imposter Syndrome', *HRD Canada* (17 May 2022), www.hcamag.com/ca/specialization/employment-law/90-of-female-employees-suffer-from-imposter-syndrome/406295, accessed October 2022

18　M Ettore, 'Why most new executives fail – and four things companies can do about it', *Forbes* (13 March 2020), www.forbes.com/sites/forbescoachescouncil/2020/03/13/why-most-new-executives-fail-and-four-things-companies-can-do-about-it, accessed December 2022

19　'Destined to break: 40% of new leaders fail within the first 18 months' (ProventusHR, March 2021), www.proventushr.com/post/shocking-40-of-new-leaders-fail-within-the-first-18-months, accessed December 2022

20　J Sundberg, 'What is the true cost of hiring a bad employee?' (Undercover Recruiter, no date), https://theundercoverrecruiter.com/infographic-what-cost-hiring-wrong-employee, accessed December 2022

21　E Suni, 'Anxiety and sleep' (Sleep Foundation, 16 September 2022), www.sleepfoundation.org/mental-health/anxiety-and-sleep, accessed December 2022; EJ Olson, 'Lack of sleep: Can it make you sick?' (Mayo Clinic, 28 November 2018), www.mayoclinic.org/diseases-conditions/insomnia/expert-answers/lack-of-sleep/faq-20057757 accessed December 2022

22　N Sinclair and P Sinclair, *Building Resilience: A prescription for tackling the global mental health crisis one step at a time* (Mind Matters, 2021), https://mindmatters.pro/wp-content/uploads/2021/06/Mind-Matters_Building-Resilience_2021.pdf, accessed December 2022

23　S Ferguson, 'Yes, mental illness can cause physical symptoms – here's why' (Healthline, 30 June 2020), www.healthline.com/health/mental-health/mental-illness-can-cause-physical-symptoms, accessed December 2022

24　'The first five years' (First Things First, no date), https://files.firstthingsfirst.org/why-early-childhood-matters/the-first-five-years, accessed December 2022

25 WL Hosch, 'Physiology' (Britannica, no date), www.
    britannica.com/science/information-theory/Physiology,
    accessed January 2023

26 M Szegedy-Maszak, 'Mysteries of the mind: Your
    unconscious is making your everyday decisions', *US
    News and World Report* (28 February 2005), http://
    faculty.fortlewis.edu/burke_b/personality/Readings/
    AdaptiveUnconscious.pdf, accessed December 2022

27 'What happens to your body during the fight or flight
    response?' (Cleveland Clinic, 9 December 2019), https://
    health.clevelandclinic.org/what-happens-to-your-body-
    during-the-fight-or-flight-response, accessed December
    2022; 'Your brain's threat system' (Mindfulness and Clinical
    Psychology Solutions, no date), https://mi-psych.com.au/
    your-brains-threat-system, accessed December 2022

28 Neuroleadership Institute, 'The 5 biggest biases that affect
    decision-making', *Your Brain at Work* (2 August 2022),
    https://neuroleadership.com/your-brain-at-work/seeds-
    model-biases-affect-decision-making, accessed October
    2022

29 Adapted from an exercise developed by Bespoke Training
    and Development: https://bespoketraining.org.uk

30 'No Man is an Island summary and analysis', (LitCharts, no
    date), www.litcharts.com/poetry/john-donne/no-man-is-
    an-island, accessed December 2022

31 D Priestley, *Key Person of Influence: The five-step method to
    become one of the most highly valued and highly paid people in
    your industry* (Rethink Press, 2014)

32 AM Elliott, CD Burton and PC Hannaford, 'Resilience does
    matter: Evidence from a 10-year cohort record linkage
    study', *BMJ Open* 4/1 (2014), https://doi.org/10.1136/
    bmjopen-2013-003917, accessed October 2022

33 CE Ackerman, 'What is resilience and why is it important
    to bounce back?', PositivePsychology.com (2019) https://
    positivepsychology.com/what-is-resilience, accessed
    October 2022

34 S Covey, *The Speed of Trust: The one thing that changes
    everything* (Free Press, 2008)

35 For more information on working with these tools, you can
    contact me through my website at www.emr-consulting.
    co.uk/contact

36 S Goldstein, 'EQ is massively more important than IQ for leaders. Here's why', *Inc.* (26 September 2017), www.inc.com/steve-goldstein/eq-is-massively-more-important-than-iq-for-leaders-heres-why.html, accessed December 2022

37 'Leadership and Emotional Intelligence Performance Accelerator' (LEIPA, no date), www.leadershapeglobal.com/Leipa, accessed December 2022. To learn more about how I work with the LEIPA assessment and development tool, contact me through my website at www.emr-consulting.co.uk/contact.

Acknowledgements

I have so many people to thank who have inspired, encouraged and supported me throughout this process:

Sam Fay, for putting the idea of becoming an author in my head in the first place, and Heather Butcher and Lisa Rabone for agreeing with Sam one fateful night in London. Your belief in me and encouragement means the world.

My husband and my children, who have put up with me being missing in action for so many weekends and evenings as I've written and rewritten this book. Your patience, love, belief and support has been unwavering.

Heather Butcher, Stephen (Shed) Shedletzsky and Alan Dunbar, for your kind words and insight into why readers should read my book.

All of my incredible clients past and present who inspire me every day to keep being better. Being part of your stories and experiences is an honour and watching you fly is a joy.

Lucy McCarraher, Joe Gregory, Bernadette Schwerdt, Joe Laredo, Abigail Willford, Kathleen Steeden and the Rethink Press team for creating an easy-to-follow guide and providing the tools, support and knowledge to help me get this book out there.

Daniel Priestley and the team at DENT Global for introducing me to what is possible when you do things right, via the KPI programme.

My amazing friends who have been so supportive but especially Lisa Foley and Louise Needham, who have done nothing but be a positive force in my life over the last few years.

And finally, the amazing, generous and incredibly supportive team of beta readers who gave me insight, ideas and feedback that have made this book better and even more helpful. Jeff Rudatt, Vicky Dvali, Amanatha King and Mr F – thank you all, I am so incredibly grateful.

The Author

 Sarah Farmer is a Global Executive Coach and Leadership Excellence Mentor, a Certified Transpersonal Leadership Coach, an NLP Business Practitioner and a Communication Skills mentor. She founded EMR Consulting in 2015 and has since trained and developed over 500 leaders, teams and entrepreneurs in a wide range of sectors to develop a stronger, powerful mindset, self-awareness and the leadership and business skills to be more productive and achieve more than they ever thought possible – with phenomenal results.

She is the founder and co-host of *The Business Brunch*, and an engaging inspirational speaker. She has a passion for supporting all of her clients to develop emotional intelligence, confidence, communication versatility, resilience and self-awareness.

Her interest in coaching and developing others started in her early teens. Her mum, who was a psychotherapist, ran her practice from home and Sarah was constantly asking her mum about the types of problems people had that brought them to counselling and how she helped them get better. She was hooked, and she believes that this is when the seed was sown and her desire to inspire and help others was set.

Sarah's first experience with personal development started with cognitive behavioural therapy at the age of thirty. She was working in a toxic environment and started to get panic attacks, which were not only embarrassingly visible, but making her ill. She found she was missing out on opportunities and potential success as she started to avoid situations when the 'panic' might set in. During this time, Sarah started to understand that her own relationship with Imposter Syndrome had started well before she was thirty, and she can trace this back to her very early childhood. She now looks back on the start of her 'personal growth journey' and, although the way she was treated at this time by her leaders was unacceptable, she can, with hindsight, thank all involved, because this is what ultimately drove her to start her own business and take more control over her future success and happiness.

Sarah's business has two principal aims: to develop leaders who know how to treat all employees with kindness, respect and dignity, so that fewer ever have to feel like she did; and to help all her clients feel empowered and powerful, building their self-belief and self-awareness so they can take control of their future, worry less, achieve more and enjoy the ride!

A self-confessed neuroscience nerd, Sarah bases everything she does on an understanding of how the brain works. She understands the value of ongoing training and continues to invest heavily in her own development. Sarah will always be working with a coach, as she knows the benefit of the mirror they hold, the questions they ask and the challenges they set, which she would not always face on her own. Great coaches help to keep her moving forward and be the very best version of herself, so she can be the best for her clients.

If you are considering investing in your own professional development, or the development of your leaders and executives, and would like to discuss how EMR Consulting may be able to help, then get in touch to schedule a call at www.emr-consulting. co.uk/contact.

⊕ www.emr-consulting.co.uk

in www.linkedin.com/in/sarah-farmer-coach

f www.facebook.com/SarahEMRConsultingLtd